Prentice Hall

LITERATURE
Timeless Voices, Timeless Themes

The British Tradition

Performance Assessment and Portfolio Management

Upper Saddle River, New Jersey
Glenview, Illinois
Needham, Massachusetts

ISBN 0-13-062397-0

1 2 3 4 5 6 7 8 9 10   05 04 03 02 01

© Prentice-Hall, Inc.

Contents

Portfolio Management

Portfolio Management

Portfolios in Your Classroom

If the classroom is a place where real and engaging work goes on, a portfolio is a device for collecting and honoring writing samples that show this work. Through the portfolio, student effort can be dignified and celebrated in a public forum that parents, students, community members, and administrators may understand and participate in. Portfolios offer the teacher and the student a reasonable way to look at real accomplishments in writing and a reliable way to assess those accomplishments. However, portfolio use comes with a price tag: It costs time and it costs effort.

Contents: Decide by Collaboration

What could a portfolio contain? This question can spark a good discussion for the teacher and the class at the beginning of the year. A group of teachers may want to address this topic as an initial staff discussion. What do we want our students to know or be able to do? Evidence of these knowings and doings should be found in the portfolio.

Design: Guidance and Choice

Teachers must be ready to give steady guidance to reluctant or inexperienced students, mentoring to others, and support to risk-takers and "gifted" writers. Using *Prentice Hall Literature,* a teacher might stress one writing mode each month or each quarter. Here is a sample plan for a middle school grade on traditional calendar year:

September: Letters, business and friendly. (Write to your summer buddy and tell how school looks so far. Write to a product manufacturer supporting or criticizing quality, packaging, advertising.)

November: Interviews (Interview an older family member about family holiday customs. Interview school staff members about changes in school since the "old days.")

January: Narratives (Brainstorm moments of personal or group experience, or create a story line of partial or complete fiction, to be published in a class literary magazine.)

March: Essays (Take a stand on some current or historical issue. Write an opinion paper for a newspaper or periodical, or a debating speech to present to the class.)

May: Poetry (Collect favorite poems and write some of your own in a similar or contrasting style. Send your poetic impressions of school, spring, current events, or friends to appropriate individuals.)

The teacher of younger students may want to include language play activities in such a schedule. The teacher of older students may want to emphasize the essay and business documents, modeling, and works of increasing complexity.

The teacher of any grade level might arrange lessons around each writing mode. *Prentice Hall Literature* anthologies present models of classic, engaging works in various modes. The Writing Workshops within each unit provide strategies and guidelines for creating each type of writing. The teacher could ask students to focus on the writing mode for a particular time period and produce at least one finished piece by a certain deadline. During March and April, for example, formal instruction could focus on the essay form, essays of all kinds, available in students' textbooks or elsewhere in the classroom could be read aloud. Others could be featured in the library. Within that period, students might produce several essays or work independently on other forms of writing. An author's circle could occur each week, with the more proficient and confident students reading their essays aloud, and others reacting to and learning from them.

Management: Checklists and Observation

What kind of management challenges does this process present? Keeping track of what students are working on is less complicated with a checklist that teacher or students fill out regularly. Periodic observation and interviews with students will help the teacher track their growth, level of engagement, and range of writing experiences. As students work and talk about their work, the teacher can assess the program of lessons needed for the group and for individuals: What writing skills, writing modes, or craft instruction does the class especially need? What reinforcements do individuals or small groups need? Quarterly reviews of the portfolio collection by students and teachers, with students doing the bulk of the record keeping, will help keep the process manageable and provide the reflective factor students need to become "owners" of the collection.

Can one portfolio serve more than one master? School districts and states may apply different standards to the contents of a portfolio. However, after meeting imposed requirements, the teacher and students might decide for themselves what kind of portfolio they want included in their class collection. They may elect to use "growth" or "development" portfolios with samples of each student's earliest to most recent writings in it. Or they may prefer "showcase" portfolios that include only each student's "best pieces." In some places, where there are specified contents for statewide assessment, classes create a large folder with developmental pieces in it and a pull-out section for official assessment.

Topics: Chosen or Imposed?

Experienced teachers know that students will work harder on projects they help design. Are there valid reasons for mixing elective and assigned pieces in a portfolio? If teachers (or districts or states) want to see how students operate under regulated conditions, they might ask from time to time that everyone write to a single prompt. There might also be writing modes on the teacher's agenda that a student chooses never to address (*e.g.*, a student may never elect to write a business letter). The teacher may feel the need to collect this kind of sample with an imposed prompt.

Portfolio Diversity: Folder or Steamer Trunk?

Should there be a record of samples other than writing? For example, should there be audiotapes, videotapes, or disks? Teachers are getting increasingly creative with these media. Should there be notations on reading experiences, artwork, research, or presentations?

Some schools are buying blank tapes and disks for each student. Recordings of dramatic readings and other oral language performances then go into the folder with the student's written work. Such additions serve to enrich the record of student experience.

Curriculum Outline

What kind of curriculum outline would help to support ongoing portfolio collections and review? Should a school teach different topics and writing modes across grades 6–12? This is a particularly important question if we want portfolio collections to reflect the rich and broad range of experiences of diverse students taught by diverse teachers. Some literature units and activities invite responses in particular writing modes; unexpected contemporary issues and events will affect some student populations and not others. An open and collegial staff atmosphere might allow teachers to assure each other that they will furnish students with certain writing opportunities at certain times.

Criteria: Back to Collaboration

How will teachers assess portfolios? Before individuals or groups begin to assess a portfolio of student writing, they must decide which aspects of writing they value. Another discussion could be productive here. Parents, teachers, and students could answer together the question "What are the qualities (criteria) of good writing?" The group will probably list organization, clarity, style, mechanics, and perhaps a few other features. Those making the decisions must take pains to be specific in defining the criteria they choose to judge by. If the group operates from an already established list, the group should take even more time to understand and accept that list. Many schools have adopted the "official" criteria (purpose, organization, details, voice, and mechanics) for their own use in classroom record keeping and reporting as well as the official statewide assessment. In *Prentice Hall Literature* (and also in this booklet) rubrics are provided for assessing each type of writing.

How should we describe the different levels students are achieving in order to assess individual work and growth? Again, teachers can generate their own descriptions of good, fair, and poor achievement. Or they can use the rubrics provided with this program.

Ultimate Goal: Student Reflection

Portfolios are useful as evidence of achievement and of growth. But to fulfill its maximum potential, the portfolio must move the student to critical thinking, analysis, and reflection as he or she chooses what to include in the portfolio. Each year, or even better, each quarter, a teacher might ask the student to choose a "best piece" of writing from the portfolio and to articulate reasons for the choice. A student involved in good classroom instruction and support will make intelligent choices, showing the kind of learning and analytical skills we want for all our students. At the end of the year, the student can be asked to select a range of "best pieces" that demonstrate good letter writing, creative writing, persuasive writing, and critical thinking. With hard work, patience, and luck, we can send our students on with a portfolio reflecting who and what they are, and we can help them feel proud of the good things they do.

Suggested Organization and Inspiration Tools

Organization Tools

1. Grid for teaching week to show status of current student projects

2. Box to keep portfolios in

3. Rack for folders of work-in-progress

4. Computers or word processors

5. 3-hole binder notebook with tabs marking sections for each student (to use for random teacher observations, samples, conference notes)

6. Benchmark collections: samples of writing illustrating strength in each criterion you value. Some samples are included in this booklet. You may wish to collect others to share with your students.

7. Timeline for topics and writing modes you will emphasize throughout the year

Inspiration Tools

1. Bank of audiences and purposes for writing

2. Names of recipients for letters or subjects of interviews

3. Connections to local media for publication, collaboration, and public relations purposes

4. Access to the Internet

5. Authentic, engaging topics for student research

6. Rigorous and engaging professional development for teachers that begins with a comprehensive look at their own literacy

7. Establishment of support networks among parent populations

Performance Assessment: Rubrics

Rubrics for Narration: Narrative Composition

Use one or both of the following sets of criteria to evaluate narrative compositions.

Criteria	Rating Scale				
	Not very				Very
How clearly does the narrative convey the significance of the incident?	1	2	3	4	5
How smoothly does the narrative move from set-up to incident to resolution?	1	2	3	4	5
How effectively do the details convey the main character's conflict?	1	2	3	4	5
How evocative is the language used to describe settings and characters?	1	2	3	4	5

	Score 4	Score 3	Score 2	Score 1
Audience and Purpose	Clearly narrates a sequence of events; explores the significance of the events in an engaging way	Narrates a sequence of events; explores the significance of the events	Describes a group of events, but the sequence is weak; alludes to the significance of the events	Vaguely describes a group of events, but the sequence is not indicated; the significance of the events is unclear
Organization	Effectively locates scenes and incidents in specific places; paces the presentation of actions to accommodate clear changes in time, space and dramatic mood	Locates scenes and incidents in specific places; paces the presentation of actions to accommodate changes in time, space and dramatic mood	Establishes settings to some extent; clearly presents actions, but inconsistently accommodates changes in time, space and dramatic mood	Does not clearly establish settings; presents actions, but fails to accommodate changes in time, space and dramatic mood
Elaboration	Uses many concrete sensory details to describe scenes, actions, and characters and to enhance the narrative	Uses some concrete sensory details to describe scenes, actions, and characters and to strengthen the narrative	Uses some concrete sensory details to describe scenes, actions, and characters	Uses few concrete sensory details to describe scenes, actions, and characters
Use of Language	Strongly and effectively uses language to narrate, create images, and shift perspectives	Effectively uses language to narrate, create images, and shift perspectives	Weakly uses language to narrate, create images, and shift perspectives	Fails to effectively use language to narrate, create images, and shift perspectives

Rubrics for Persuasion: Persuasive Composition

Use one or both of the following sets of criteria to evaluate persuasive compositions.

Criteria	Rating Scale				
	Not very				Very
How clearly is the writer's position stated?	1	2	3	4	5
How effectively is the presentation of arguments organized?	1	2	3	4	5
How appropriately do arguments and examples fit the audience and purpose?	1	2	3	4	5
How well are arguments reasoned?	1	2	3	4	5
How strong are the language and phrasing techniques?	1	2	3	4	5

	Score 4	Score 3	Score 2	Score 1
Audience and Purpose	Presents a clear opinion that is strongly supported by convincing and persuasive techniques suited to the audience	Presents an opinion that is supported by somewhat convincing and persuasive techniques suited to the audience	Presents a somewhat vague opinion with weak persuasive techniques that are not well suited to the audience	Presents a vague opinion that is not supported by persuasive techniques
Organization	Structures ideas and arguments in a sustained, persuasive, and sophisticated way	Structures ideas and arguments in a sustained and persuasive way	Structures ideas and arguments in a somewhat persuasive way	Fails to structure ideas and arguments in a persuasive way
Elaboration	Supports ideas and arguments with precise, convincing, and relevant examples; provides many specific, well-elaorated reasons	Supports ideas and arguments with convincing and relevant examples; provides some specific reasons	Supports ideas and arguments with some relevant examples; provides one or two specific reasons	Does not support ideas and arguments with reasonable or relevant examples; provides no specific reasons
Use of Language	Does not include any empty or hedging words; introduces few, if any, mechanical and grammatical errors	Includes a few empty or hedging words; introduces a few mechanical and grammatical errors	Includes a noticeable number of empty or hedging words; introduces some mechanical and grammatical errors	Includes many empty or hedging words; introduces many mechanical and grammatical errors

Rubrics for Narration: Reflective Composition

Use one or both of the following sets of criteria to evaluate reflective compositions.

Criteria	Rating Scale				
	Not very				Very
How well does the essay convey the general belief on which it is based?	1	2	3	4	5
How balanced is the essay between incidents and generalizations?	1	2	3	4	5
How clearly are connections between incidents and generalizations established?	1	2	3	4	5
How effectively and succinctly are the incidents presented?	1	2	3	4	5
How well is tone established through word choice?	1	2	3	4	5

	Score 4	Score 3	Score 2	Score 1
Audience and Purpose	Clearly explores the significance of a personal experience or condition; effectively presents an insight about life	Explores the significance of a personal experience or condition; clearly presents an insight about life	Addresses the significance of a personal experience or condition; alludes to an insight about life	Vaguely describes a personal experience; fails to present an insight about life
Organization	Narrates a sequence of events that clearly forms the basis of an insight; maintains a balance in describing specific incidents and relating them to more general and abstract ideas	Narrates a sequence of events that clearly conveys an insight; describes specific incidents and relates them to more general and abstract ideas	Narrates a sequence of events that vaguely relates to an insight; attempts to connect the essay's insight to the specific incidents described	Includes some events that indicate a sense of an insight; makes one or two associations among the specific incidents described
Elaboration	Effectively uses rhetorical strategies; draws clear comparisons between specific incidents and broader themes	Uses rhetorical strategies; draws comparisons between specific incidents and broader themes	Uses rhetorical strategies somewhat; draws a few comparisons between specific incidents and broader themes	Uses rhetorical strategies ineffectively or not at all; vaguely compares specific incidents to a broader theme
Use of Language	Uses language to consistently enhance subtlety of meaning and tone; introduces few, if any, errors	Uses language to convey some subtlety of meaning and tone; introduces few, if any, errors	Uses language to convey basic meanings; includes some mechanical and grammatical errors	Does not present clear meanings; includes many mechanical and grammatical errors

Rubrics for Cover Letter and Résumé

Use one or both of the following sets of criteria to evaluate cover letters and resumes.

Criteria	Rating Scale				
	Not very				Very
How appropriate is the language and tone of the cover letter?	1	2	3	4	5
How clearly does the letter summarize the writer's intent and achievements?	1	2	3	4	5
How accurately does the letter follow standard letter format?	1	2	3	4	5
How well does the résumé convey job and life experiences relevant to this particular job?	1	2	3	4	5
How clearly is the résumé organized?	1	2	3	4	5
How direct and dynamic is the language of the resume?	1	2	3	4	5

	Score 4	Score 3	Score 2	Score 1
Audience and Purpose	Formally and clearly provides purposeful information; addresses the intended audience appropriately	Formally provides purposeful information; addresses the intended audience appropriately	Formally provides information; does not clearly address the intended audience	Uses informal language; does not address the intended audience appropriately
Organization	Follows a conventional style for business documents; uses a uniform font and spacing; effectively organizes information	Follows a conventional style for business documents; uses a uniform font and spacing; logically organizes information	Follows some formatting for business writing; logically organizes most information	Uses an inappropriate format for business writing; inconsistently or randomly presents information
Elaboration	Clearly states and supports the reasons for writing; provides pertinent and appropriate information	States and supports the reasons for writing; provides appropriate information	States a reason for writing, but needs more support for it; provides mostly appropriate information	Fails to state the reasons for writing; does not provide enough appropriate information
Use of Language	Uses widely varied levels, patterns, and types of language to achieve intended effects and aid comprehension; introduces few, if any, mechanical errors	Uses varied levels, patterns, and types of language to achieve intended effects and aid comprehension; introduces a few mechanical errors	Uses some variety in levels, patterns, and types of language; introduces some mechanical errors	Uses little variety in levels, patterns, and types of language; introduces many mechanical errors

Rubrics for Research: Historical Investigation

Use one or both of the following sets of criteria to evaluate historical investigations.

Criteria	Rating Scale				
	Not very				Very
How clearly does the introduction establish background and purpose?	1	2	3	4	5
How strong and varied are the source materials?	1	2	3	4	5
How effectively are source materials analyzed and compared?	1	2	3	4	5
How well are quotations and paraphrases used to make points?	1	2	3	4	5
How completely and accurately presented are citations and bibliography?	1	2	3	4	5

	Score 4	Score 3	Score 2	Score 1
Audience and Purpose	Examines several historical records of a single event; analyzes critical relationships between elements of a research topic	Examines several historical records of a single event; addresses critical relationships between elements of a research topic	Reviews one or two historical records of an event; vaguely addresses critical relationships between elements of a research topic	Draws on only one historical record of an event; does not adequately address critical relationships between elements of a research topic
Organization	Presents all relevant perspectives; considers the validity and reliability of sources	Presents multiple perspectives; addresses the validity and reliability of sources	Presents only one perspective; does not consider the validity and reliability of sources	Vaguely presents a perspective; does not consider the validity and reliability of sources
Elaboration	Uses strong rhetoric for support; clearly explains reasons for similarities and differences of primary and secondary source information	Uses rhetoric for support; explains reasons for similarities and differences of primary and secondary source information	Attempts to use rhetoric to support the main idea; does not adequately explain the reasons for similarities and differences of source information	Does not use rhetorical strategies; does not explain the reasons for similarities and differences of source information
Use of Language	Includes a formal and complete bibliography; introduces few errors	Includes a complete bibliography; introduces a few errors	Includes an incomplete bibliography; introduces some errors	Does not include a formal bibliography; introduces many errors

Rubrics for Multimedia Script

Use one or both of the following sets of criteria to evaluate multimedia scripts.

Criteria	Rating Scale
	Not very Very
How quickly is your purpose or topic made clear?	1 2 3 4 5
How smoothly does the text lead into the various media sources?	1 2 3 4 5
How interesting, varied, and appropriate are the media sources?	1 2 3 4 5
How effectively are transitions used to move from one segment to the next?	1 2 3 4 5
How strong and memorable is the ending?	1 2 3 4 5

	Score 4	Score 3	Score 2	Score 1
Audience and Purpose	Generates a clear and creative presentation; uses the audience's responses to revise the script accordingly	Generates a clear and complete presentation; uses the audience's responses to revise the script	Generates a complete presentation; notes the audience's responses and revises somewhat accordingly	Generates an incomplete presentation; fails to note the audience's responses
Organization	Structures ideas in a sustained and sophisticated way; uses and edits media aptly and monitors for quality	Structures ideas consistently; uses and edits media aptly and monitors for quality	Structures ideas somewhat consistently; uses media but quality is inconsistent	Structure ideas inconsistently; uses media inappropriately and quality is inconsistent
Elaboration	Combines text, images, and sound skillfully; uses precise and relevant media examples to enhance ideas	Combines text, images, and sound skillfully; uses media to support ideas with relevant examples	Combines text, images, and sound; uses media to support ideas with some examples	Uses text, images, and sound, but they are not combined or used effectively
Use of Language	Uses language in natural, fresh, and vivid ways to establish a specific tone; follows a distinct script format	Uses language in natural ways to establish a specific tone; follows an appropriate script format	Uses language in somewhat natural ways, but an inconsistent tone is achieved; follows a vague script format	Uses language in ineffective ways, and an inconsistent tone is achieved; script format is unrecognizable

Rubrics for Narration: Autobiographical Writing

Use one or both of the following sets of criteria to evaluate autobiographical narratives.

Criteria	Rating Scale Not very				Very
How well established is the writer as the main character?	1	2	3	4	5
How significant and clear is the sequence of events?	1	2	3	4	5
How well is the action paced to accommodate shifts in time and mood?	1	2	3	4	5
How powerfully are concrete and sensory details used to describe events?	1	2	3	4	5
How well is interior monologue used to convey the thoughts and feelings of the writer?	1	2	3	4	5

	Score 4	Score 3	Score 2	Score 1
Audience and Purpose	Contains details that engage the audience	Contains details appropriate for an audience	Contains few details that appeal to an audience	Is not written for a specific audience
Organization	Presents events that create an interesting narrative; told from a consistent point of view	Presents sequence of events; told from a specific point of view	Presents a confusing sequence of events; contains a point of view that is inconsistent	Presents no logical order; is told from no consistent point of view
Elaboration	Contains details that create vivid characters; contains dialogue that develops characters and plot	Contains details that develop character and describe setting; contains dialogue	Contains characters and setting; contains some dialogue	Contains few or no details to develop characters or setting; no dialogue provided
Use of Language	Uses language to create a tone; contains no errors in grammar, punctuation, or spelling	Uses vivid words; contains few errors in grammar, punctuation, and spelling	Uses clichés and trite expressions; contains some errors in grammar, punctuation, and spelling	Uses uninspired words; has many errors in grammar, punctuation, and spelling

Rubrics for Narration: Short Story

Use one or both of the following sets of criteria to evaluate short stories.

Criteria	Rating Scale				
	Not very				Very
How effectively does the story show a change for growth in the main character?	1	2	3	4	5
How apparent and clear is the story's conflict?	1	2	3	4	5
How clearly and vividly is the setting depicted?	1	2	3	4	5
How well does the plot build to a climax?	1	2	3	4	5
How well is the theme developed?	1	2	3	4	5
How strong are the sensory details of the story's descriptions?	1	2	3	4	5

	Score 4	Score 3	Score 2	Score 1
Audience and Purpose	Contains details that create a tone to engage the audience	Contains details and language that appeal to an audience	Contains few details that contribute to its purpose or appeal to an audience	Contains no purpose; is not written for a specific audience
Organization	Presents events that create an interesting, clear narrative; told from a consistent point of view	Presents sequence of events; told from a specific point of view	Presents a confusing sequence of events; contains inconsistent points of view	Presents no logical order; is told from no consistent point of view
Elaboration	Contains details that provide insight into character; contains dialogue that reveals characters and furthers the plot	Contains details and dialogue that develop character	Contains characters and setting; contains some dialogue	Contains few or no details to develop characters or setting; no dialogue provided
Use of Language	Uses word choice and tone to reveal story's theme; contains no errors in grammar, punctuation, or spelling	Uses interesting and fresh word choices; contains few errors in grammar, punctuation, and spelling	Uses clichés and trite expressions; contains some errors in grammar, punctuation, and spelling	Uses uninspired word choices; has many errors in grammar, punctuation, and spelling

Rubrics for Description

Use one or both of the following sets of criteria to evaluate descriptions.

Criteria	Rating Scale				
	Not very				Very
How clearly and consistently is the description organized?	1	2	3	4	5
How effectively are details used to create imagery?	1	2	3	4	5
How evocative is the figurative language?	1	2	3	4	5
How well are shifting perspectives portrayed?	1	2	3	4	5

	Score 4	Score 3	Score 2	Score 1
Audience and Purpose	Contains details that work together to create a single, dominant impression of the topic	Creates through use of details a dominant impression of the topic	Contains extraneous details that detract from the main impression	Contains details that are unfocused and create no dominant impression
Organization	Is organized consistently, logically, and effectively	Is organized consistently	Is organized, but not consistently	Is disorganized and confusing
Elaboration	Contains creative use of sensory language	Contains much sensory language	Contains some sensory language	Contains no sensory language
Use of Language	Contains sensory language that appeals to the five senses; contains no errors in grammar, punctuation, or spelling	Contains some sensory language; contains few errors in grammar, punctuation, and spelling	Contains some sensory language, but it appeals to only one or two of the senses; contains some errors in grammar, punctuation, and spelling	Contains no sensory language; contains many errors in grammar, punctuation, and spelling

Rubrics for Persuasion: Persuasive Speech

Use one or both of the following sets of criteria to evaluate persuasive speeches.

Criteria	Rating Scale				
	Not very				Very
How clearly stated is the issue?	1	2	3	4	5
How logically and effectively is the speech organized?	1	2	3	4	5
How clear and well supported with evidence is the writer's opinion?	1	2	3	4	5
How well does the writer address listener's or readers' concerns and counterclaims?	1	2	3	4	5

	Score 4	Score 3	Score 2	Score 1
Audience and Purpose	Chooses highly effective words; clearly focuses on persuasive task	Chooses effective words; focuses on persuasive task	Occasionally uses effective words; is minimally focused on persuasive task	Poor word choice shows lack of attention to persuasive task
Organization	Uses clear, consistent organizational strategy	Uses clear organizational strategy with occasional inconsistencies	Uses inconsistent organizational strategy and illogical presentation	Lacks organizational strategy; gives confusing presentation
Elaboration	Contains specific, well-elaborated reasons that provide convincing support for the writer's position	Contains two or more moderately elaborated reasons in support of the writer's position	Contains several reasons, but few are elaborated	Contains no specific reasons
Use of Language	Contains no empty or hedging words; makes no errors in grammar, spelling, and punctuation	Contains few empty or hedging words; makes few errors in grammar, spelling, and punctuation	Contains some empty and hedging words; makes errors in grammar, spelling, and punctuation	Contains many empty or hedging words; makes many errors in grammar, spelling, and punctuation

Rubrics for Persuasion: Advertisement

Use one or both of the following sets of criteria to evaluate advertisements.

Criteria	Not very	Rating Scale			Very
How clever and purposeful is the slogan?	1	2	3	4	5
How effectively has the advertisement's audience been targeted?	1	2	3	4	5
How effective are the layout and design elements?	1	2	3	4	5
How convincingly do words and images combine to support a position?	1	2	3	4	5

	Score 4	Score 3	Score 2	Score 1
Audience and Purpose	Presents effective slogan; clearly addresses persuasive task	Presents good slogan; addresses persuasive task	Presents slogan; minimally addresses persuasive task	Does not present slogan; shows lack of attention to persuasive task
Organization	Uses clear, consistent organizational strategy; clearly presents key ideas	Uses clear organizational strategy with few inconsistencies	Uses inconsistent organizational strategy; creates illogical presentation	Demonstrates lack of organizational strategy; creates confusing presentation
Elaboration	Successfully combines words and images to provide convincing, unified support for a position	Combines words and images to provide unified support for a position	Includes some words or images that detract from a position	Uses words and images that do not support a position
Use of Language	Successfully communicates an idea through clever use of language; includes very few mechanical errors	Conveys an idea through adequate use of language; includes few mechanical errors	Misuses language and lessens impact of ideas; includes many mechanical errors	Demonstrates poor use of language and confuses meaning; includes many mechanical errors

Rubrics for Exposition: Comparison-and-Contrast Essay

Use one or both of the following sets of criteria to evaluate comparison-and contrast essays.

Criteria	Rating Scale				
	Not very				Very
How apparent is a thesis statement?	1	2	3	4	5
How clearly identified are the subjects?	1	2	3	4	5
How sufficiently have details supported each statement about the similarities and differences between the subjects?	1	2	3	4	5
How well do transitions organize the relationships between sujects?	1	2	3	4	5

	Score 4	Score 3	Score 2	Score 1
Audience and Purpose	Clearly provides a reason for a comparison-contrast analysis	Adequately provides a reason for a comparison-contrast analysis	Provides a reason for a comparison-contrast analysis	Does not provide a reason for a comparison-contrast analysis
Organization	Clearly presents information in a consistent organization best suited to the topic	Presents information using an organization suited to the topic	Chooses an organization not suited to comparison and contrast	Shows a lack of organizational strategy
Elaboration	Elaborates several ideas with facts, details, or examples; links all information to comparison and contrast	Elaborates most ideas with facts, details, or examples; links most information to comparison and contrast	Does not elaborate all ideas; does not link some details to comparison and contrast	Does not provide facts or examples to support a comparison and contrast
Use of Language	Demonstrates excellent sentence and vocabulary variety; includes very few mechanical errors	Demonstrates adequate sentence and vocabulary variety; includes few mechanical errors	Demonstrates repetitive use of sentence structure and vocabulary; includes many mechanical errors	Demonstrates poor use of language; generates confusion; includes many mechanical errors

Rubrics for Exposition: Cause-and-Effect Essay

Use one or both of the following sets of criteria to evaluate cause-and-effect essays.

Criteria	Rating Scale Not very Very				
How clearly does the thesis statement identify the purpose of the essay?	1	2	3	4	5
How successfully are causes and effects explained and related to one another?	1	2	3	4	5
How consistently and appropriately are ideas organized?	1	2	3	4	5
How well supported are explanations and ideas?	1	2	3	4	5
How clearly do transitions connect ideas?	1	2	3	4	5

	Score 4	Score 3	Score 2	Score 1
Audience and Purpose	Consistently targets an audience; clearly identifies purpose in thesis statement	Targets an audience; identifies purpose in thesis statement	Misses a target audience by including a wide range of word choice and details; presents no clear purpose	Addresses no specific audience or purpose
Organization	Presents a clear, consistent organizational strategy to show cause and effect	Presents a clear organizational strategy with occasional inconsistencies shows cause and effect	Presents an inconsistent organizational strategy; creates illogical presentation of causes and effects	Demonstrates a lack of organizational strategy; creates a confusing presentation
Elaboration	Successfully links causes with effects; fully elaborates connections among ideas	Links causes with effects; elaborates connections among most ideas	Links some causes with some effects; elaborates connections among most ideas	Develops and elaborates no links between causes and effects
Use of Language	Uses words precisely; presents very few mechanical errors	Uses words precisely; presents few mechanical errors	Contains some imprecise words; presents many mechanical errors	Demonstrates poor use of words; presents many mechanical errors

Rubrics for Exposition: Problem-Solution Essay

Use one or both of the following sets of criteria to evaluate problem-solution-essays.

Criteria	Rating Scale				
	Not very				Very
How clearly is the problem stated?	1	2	3	4	5
How practical and well supported is the suggested solution?	1	2	3	4	5
How effective are facts, statistics, and details that illustrate the problem and solution?	1	2	3	4	5
How well does the language address the audience's knowledge level?	1	2	3	4	5
How appropriate is the essay's organizational stategy?	1	2	3	4	5

	Score 4	Score 3	Score 2	Score 1
Audience and Purpose	Contains language and details to engage audience and accomplish purpose	Contains language and details appropriate for audience and that help contribute to overall effect	Contains some language and details not suited for audience; contains some details that detract from purpose	Contains language and details that are not geared for a particular audience; has an unclear purpose
Organization	Is organized consistently, logically, and effectively	Has consistent organization	Has inconsistent organization	Is disorganized and confusing
Elaboration	Has a solution that is clearly laid out, along with details that support or explain it	Has a solution that is supported with details	Has a stated solution, but contains few details to support it	Has unclear solution, and no details are given to support it
Use of Language	Contains precise words and no redundancies; contains no errors in grammar, punctuation, or spelling	Contains effective words and few redundancies; contains few errors in grammar, punctuation, and spelling	Contains few precise words and some redundancies; contains some errors in grammar, punctuation, and spelling	Contains imprecise words and many redundancies; contains many errors in grammar, punctuation, and spelling

Rubrics for Research: Documented Essay

Use one or both of the following sets of criteria to evaluate documented essays.

Criteria	Not very	Rating Scale			Very
How clear and focused is the thesis statement?	1	2	3	4	5
How effectively is the audience and purpose addressed?	1	2	3	4	5
How clear is the essay's organizational strategy?	1	2	3	4	5
How effectively are documented sources used?	1	2	3	4	5
How clearly does research information relate to the topic of the essay?	1	2	3	4	5

	Score 4	Score 3	Score 2	Score 1
Audience and Purpose	Consistently targets a unique audience; clearly identifies purpose in thesis statement	Targets a specific audience; identifies purpose in thesis statement	Misses target audience by including too many details; presents no clear thesis	Addresses no specific audience or purpose
Organization	Presents a clear, consistent organizational strategy	Presents a clear organizational strategy with few inconsistencies	Presents an inconsistent organizational strategy; creates illogical presentation	Demonstrates a lack of organization; creates confusing presentation
Elaboration	Supports thesis statement with several documented sources; elaborates all main points	Supports thesis statement with some documented sources; elaborates most points	Supports the thesis statement with one documented source; elaborates some points	Provides no documented sources; does not provide thesis
Use of Language	Clearly integrates researched information into the writing; presents very few mechanical errors	Integrates most researched information into the writing; presents very few mechanical errors	Does not integrate researched information into the writing; presents many mechanical errors	Demonstrates poor use of language; presents many mechanical errors

Rubrics for Research: Research Paper

Use one or both of the following sets of criteria to evaluate research papers.

Criteria	Not very	Rating Scale			Very
How clear and focused is the thesis statement?	1	2	3	4	5
How effectively does the writer use primary and secondary sources?	1	2	3	4	5
How strong is the paper's organizational strategy?	1	2	3	4	5
How accurate and complete is the bibliography?	1	2	3	4	5
How effectively do visual aids present and enhance the delivery of information?	1	2	3	4	5

	Score 4	Score 3	Score 2	Score 1
Audience and Purpose	Focuses on a clearly stated thesis, starting from a well-framed question; gives complete citations	Focuses on a clearly stated thesis; gives citations	Focuses mainly on the chosen topic; gives some citations	Presents information without a clear focus; few or no citations
Organization	Presents information in logical order, emphasizing details of central importance	Presents information in logical order	Presents information logically, but organization is poor in places	Presents information in a scattered, disorganized manner
Elaboration	Draws clear conclusions from information gathered from multiple sources	Draws conclusions from information gathered from multiple sources	Explains and interprets some information	Presents information with little or no interpretation or synthesis
Use of Language	Shows overall clarity and fluency; contains few mechanical errors	Shows good sentence variety; contains some errors in spelling, punctuation, or usage	Uses awkward or overly simple sentences; contains many mechanical errors	Contains incomplete thoughts and many mechanical errors

Rubrics for Response to Literature

Use one or both of the following sets of criteria to evaluate responses to literature.

Criteria	Not very		Rating Scale		Very
How well have the significant ideas of the literary work been addressed?	1	2	3	4	5
How well has the writer explored the use of imagery, language, universal themes, and unique aspects of the text?	1	2	3	4	5
How well supported with accurate and detailed references to the text are important ideas?	1	2	3	4	5
How effectively has the writer incorprated personal ideas?	1	2	3	4	5

	Score 4	Score 3	Score 2	Score 1
Audience and Purpose	Presents sufficient background on the work(s); presents the writer's reactions forcefully	Presents background on the work(s); presents the writer's reactions clearly	Presents some background on the work(s); presents the writer's reactions at points	Presents little or no background on the work(s); presents few of the writer's reactions
Organization	Presents points in logical order, smoothly connecting them to the overall focus	Presents points in logical order and connects them to the overall focus	Organizes points poorly in places; connects some points to an overall focus	Presents information in a scattered, disorganized manner
Elaboration	Supports reactions and evaluations with elaborated reasons and well-chosen examples	Supports reactions and evaluations with specific reasons and examples	Supports some reactions and evaluations with reasons and examples	Offers little support for reactions and evaluations
Use of Language	Shows overall clarity and fluency; uses precise, evaluative words; makes few mechanical errors	Shows good sentence variety; uses some precise evaluative terms; makes some mechanical errors	Uses awkward or overly simple sentence structures and vague evaluative terms; makes many mechanical errors	Presents incomplete thoughts; makes mechanical errors that cause confusion

Rubrics for Writing for Assessment

Use one or both of the following sets of criteria to evaluate writing for assessment.

Criteria	Rating Scale				
	Not very				Very
How well has the writing prompt been addressed?	1	2	3	4	5
How clear and focused is the thesis statement?	1	2	3	4	5
How sufficiently do details support the thesis?	1	2	3	4	5
How logical and consistent is the organizational strategy throughout the essay?	1	2	3	4	5
How appropriate is the use of language?	1	2	3	4	5

	Score 4	Score 3	Score 2	Score 1
Audience and Purpose	Uses appropriately formal diction; clearly addresses writing prompt	Uses mostly formal diction; adequately addresses writing prompt	Uses some informal diction; addresses writing prompt	Uses inappropriately informal diction; does not address writing prompt
Organization	Presents a clear, consistent organizational strategy	Presents a clear organizational strategy with few inconsistencies	Presents an inconsistent organizational strategy	Shows a lack of organizational strategy
Elaboration	Provides several ideas to support the thesis; elaborates each idea; links all information to thesis	Provides several ideas to support the thesis; elaborates most ideas with facts, details, or examples; links most information to thesis	Provides some ideas to support the thesis; does not elaborate some ideas; does not link some details to thesis	Provides no thesis; does not elaborate ideas
Use of Language	Uses excellent sentence and vocabulary variety; includes very few mechanical errors	Uses adequate sentence and vocabulary variety; includes few mechanical errors	Uses repetitive use of sentence structure and vocabulary; includes many mechanical errors	Demonstrates poor use of language; generates confusion; includes many mechanical errors

Rubric for Analyzing Persuasive Techniques

Use the following rubric to assess analyzing persuasive techniques.

Rating System

+ = excellent   ✓ = average   — = weak

Content
Recognizes purpose _____
Develops expectations _____
Categorizes persuasive speech according to type _____
Assesses appropriateness of evidence _____
Assesses pertinence of proof _____
Analyzes reasoning for flaws and weaknesses _____

Delivery
Interprets and evaluates presentation strategies _____
Critiques diction and syntax in relation to purpose _____
Identifies logical fallacies _____
Listens critically for clarity, quality, effectiveness, and general coherence _____
Listens critically for emotional appeals, rhetorical questions, and deductive arguments _____
Analyzes the techniques used for the particular audience _____

Analysis Summary
The types of persuasive techniques are identified and evaluated _____
Logical fallacies are taken into account _____
An evaluation of clarity, quality, effectiveness, and general coherence is made _____
Sound reasoning is used to make a judgment about the persuasive techniques _____

Rubric for Critiquing Persuasive Arguments

Use the following rubric to assess critiquing persuasive arguments.

Rating System

+ = excellent	✓ = average	— = weak

Content
Analyzes persuasive techniques _____
Identifies use of attack *ad hominem*, false causality, and red herring _____
Evaluates techniques used in oral addresses _____
Challenges generalizations _____

Delivery
Analyzes argument structure _____
Listens critically to the organization of ideas _____
Listens critically for persuasive devices and fallacious arguments _____
Identifies circular reasoning, overgeneralization, and bandwagon effect _____
Listens critically for diction and syntax in relation to the purpose of the argument _____

Critique Summary
The argument is broken down into parts for analysis _____
A decision is made as to whether the argument is accurate or faulty _____
A decision is made as to whether the argument is strong or weak _____
An evaluation of clarity, quality, effectiveness, and general coherence is made _____
Sound reasoning is used to critique the argument _____

Rubric for Analyzing Advertising

Use the following rubric to assess analyzing advertising.

Rating System		
+ = excellent	✓ = average	— = weak

Content
Recognizes the persuasive message and techniques used to present it _____
Identifies the type of media used to convey the persuasive message _____
Identifies purpose of the message and determines the targeted audience _____

Delivery
Identifies advertising elements such as concept, hook, charged language, characters, special effects, and mood _____
Assesses purpose and impact of advertising elements _____
Identifies and assesses cultural values illustrated in the advertisement _____
Evaluates individual visual elements for appropriateness and contributing factors _____

Analysis Summary
Tone, image, cultural values, and purpose are taken into account _____
A decision as to whether the advertisement's purpose had been achieved is made _____
An overall conclusion is drawn about the advertisement _____

Rubric for Media Analysis of the News

Use the following rubric to evaluate media analyses of the news.

Rating System		
+ = excellent	✓ = average	— = weak

Content
Analyzes explicit influences _____
Analyzes implicit influences _____
Identifies editorials _____
Recognizes opinion forums _____
Questions sources of information _____
Weighs objectivity and subjectivity _____

Delivery
Analyzes structure _____
Considers the impact of the story's placement in a broadcast _____
Considers omissions and inclusions of information _____
Compares new sources _____
Evaluates timeliness of news coverage _____

Analysis Summary
Media sources are analyzed _____
Information is interpreted _____
The media's communication methods are analyzed _____
Sound reasoning is used to make a judgment about the news conveyed,
as well as the media's influence _____

Rubric for Delivering an Autobiographical Presentation

Use the following rubric to evaluate autobiographical presentations.

Rating System		
+ = excellent	✓ = average	— = weak

Content
Establishes and maintains context _____
Uses elements such as rhetorical questions, parallel structure, concrete images, figurative language, characterization, irony, and dialogue _____
Illustrates personal relationship to the story _____
Draws a conclusion _____

Delivery
Uses appropriate verbal techniques _____
Uses appropriate nonverbal techniques _____
Uses an organizational structure that matches purpose _____
Use sound or visual effects, graphics, and background music to enhance or complement the presentation _____
Achieves a focused and coherent presentation _____

Presentation Summary
Attitude toward presentation is apparent and appropriate _____
Attitude toward the audience is apparent and appropriate _____
Preparation is evident and thorough _____
Organization is discernible and effective _____

Rubric for Delivering a Persuasive Speech

Use the following rubric to evaluate persuasive speeches.

Rating System		
+ = excellent	✓ = average	— = weak

Content
Establishes and maintains context _____
Uses a basic type of persuasive speech: proposition of fact, value, problem, or policy _____
Distinguishes between and uses of logical arguments, such as inductive and deductive reasoning or syllogisms and analogies _____
Modifies content to fit the audience's knowledge _____

Delivery
Uses appropriate verbal techniques _____
Uses appropriate nonverbal techniques _____
Uses an organizational structure that matches purpose _____
Uses logical, ethical, and emotional appeals that enhance the selected tone and purpose _____
Achieves a focused and coherent presentation _____

Presentation Summary
Attitude toward speech is apparent and appropriate _____
Attitude toward the audience is apparent and appropriate _____
Effective persuasive techniques are used _____
Preparation is evident and thorough _____
Organization is discernible and effective _____

Listening and Speaking Progress Chart: Teacher Observation

Directions to the teacher: This chart is designed to help you track the progress of students' listening and speaking behavior. Write the students' names in the first column. Use the Key to record your observations for each behavior. Share your observations with students to help them recognize how their listening and speaking skills have progressed and to help them set goals for improving.

Key   **P** = Proficient   **I** = Improving   **N** = Needs Attention

Progress Chart: Listening

Student's Name	Pays attention.	Listens with a purpose.	Is polite and does not interrupt.	Responds appropriately.	Asks questions clarify ideas.

Listening and Speaking Progress Chart: Teacher Observation

Directions to the teacher: This chart is designed to help you track the progress of students' listening and speaking behavior. Write the students' names in the first column. Use the Key to record your observations for each behavior. Share your observations with students to help them recognize how their listening and speaking skills have progressed and to help them set goals for improving.

Key   **P** = Proficient   **I** = Improving   **N** = Needs Attention

Progress Chart: Speaking

Student's Name	Enjoys speaking to a group.	Appears calm and confident.	Is prepared and knows material.	Uses body language and gestures effectively.	Uses visual aids effectively.

Performance Assessment: Scoring Models

The models of student work that follow are scored 1, 2, 3, or 4. In addition to rubrics, you may use these models as a guide when assessing your students' work.

Scoring Model for Narration: Autobiographical Narrative

Score 4

This writer presents an engaging, well-developed autobiographical narrative that develops character and plot and offers clear insights.

Strong Points:

1. Interesting and engaging lead
2. Suspense and climax
3. Clear insight about an experience
4. Events organized to create an interesting narrative
5. Rich details and dialogue that develops narrative
6. Varied sentence structure
7. Develops character and plot
8. No errors of grammar, punctuation, or spelling

A Close Call

After making several attempts to hit the field hockey ball out of the over-grown grass, I finally made enough effort for it to reach Charisa, who launched the ball to Vivien. I watched as Vivien ran to catch up with the ball that zoomed past her. Just watching her was making me tired.

"It's unbearably hot out here!" I exclaimed. It was no hotter than any other August day in Oklahoma, but today it seemed intolerable. "Let's take a break to get some water." We all agreed.

The van Vivien had driven to the field was parked nearby. Laughing and horse playing around, we all got water and then started loading our stuff into the van. As Charisa went to open the passenger door, Vivien backed up, just a little. When she stopped again, Charisa stepped onto the front bumper of Vivien's van, facing us with her hands on the hood. Vivien started to drive.

I suddenly had an uneasy feeling. A wash of dread came over me as if some-one were saying in a commanding tone, "Hey, this is a bad idea." I dismissed the feeling as paranoia.

"Hey, Vivien, drive slow, we don't want Charisa to get hurt."

"Yeah, I know," she responded in her Boston accent. "I'll drive slow."

A split second later, Vivien had stopped the van and Charisa was no longer on the front. Vivian wasn't driving fast but the force of stopping hard had caused Charisa to lose her balance and fall off the front. Immediately, I jumped out of the side of the van and ran over to Charisa. Vivien followed. A million things rushed through my mind.

Oh, no. Oh, please let her be OK.

"Charisa," I yelled, "Charisa, wake up. Open your eyes."

Oh, please let her wake up. Blood was pouring out of her ear. *Oh, dear, what am I supposed to do? I wish I had paid more attention in school.* A crowd was gathering around us, drawn from the neighborhood.

"I called the paramedics," said one man holding a cell phone. "How old is she?"

"Fifteen," I responded.

One of the women in the crowd started taking her blood pressure, ex-plaining that she was a nurse.

"280 over 110!" she exclaimed.

"Is that bad?" *Why didn't I pay attention in school?*

"Extremely bad," said the other women.

What should I do? What do they do on TV? Keep her conscious. That's the key. That's what you always hear. What's taking the ambulance so long? It should be here by now.

The paramedics finally arrived after what seemed like an eternity. As they were loading Charisa onto the stretcher, I called Charisa's mom. My hands were shaking uncontrollably.

"Hello, this is Melisia. Well, . . ." *How do I start? I don't want to freak her out. This is the phone call that no one ever wants to make.* "Charisa has been in an accident. She's hurt."

"Oh, no! What happened?"

I didn't know what to do or say, so I spoke from the heart. My inner voice was whispering into my ear the whole time, telling me what to do, what to say.

"Charisa is going to be OK. City Hospital will take good care of her. They have the best trauma center around." I think the words brought more comfort to me than her. I got off the phone and handed it back to the owner. I had a moment to reflect. It all caught up with me.

I could feel a breeze on my face. I was staring at nothing—just blank. *I think I'm going to be sick. And my knees—they won't stop shaking.*

A lot happened in the days that followed. Charisa's condition went from critical to serious. Finally, she regained consciousness. The worst of it was over. She had a long, slow recovery, but we were all so lucky. I think I learned more than everyone else. I learned that we aren't invincible; we are fragile, and we can be taken from this world in an instant. And I learned always to trust my instincts.

Scoring Model for Narration: Autobiographical Narrative

Score 3

This writer presents a clear, well-organized autobiographical narrative with some insight.

Strong Points:

1. Clear reason for writing
2. Clear sequence of events
3. Appropriate details that develop character and describe setting
4. Sentence variety

Problem Points:

1. More biographical than autobiographical content
2. Lacks dialogue
3. Some spelling and punctuation errors

A Moment in the Life of Mai-Ling

My on-going search for the perfect picture of my sister turned into hours. I had come across an ancient dusty box in the back of my sister's closet, filled with what seemed like millions of pictures. I had almost given up looking when my search suddenly came to an end. There, lying right in front of my face, was the image of my sister Mai-Ling smiling back at me. It was a picture I had never seen before. It captured in one "flash" her bravery, strength, and true identity.

I was completely astonished to see *my sister*—who refused to ride in elevators because of her fear of heights—repelling down a steep mountain, with only a single rope to keep her from falling. I sat back in revery, vividly remembering that weekend. I had been as excited as she was about her leaving for two whole days. She asked me if I would miss her, and when it took me more than a second to answer, she stuck her tongue out at me and walked away. Before she left, though, I said good-bye and we hugged.

Sunday when we pulled into the parking lot to pick her up, there she was, sunburned, sleepy and sore from head to toe. That night, I tried to talk to her about her weekend without sounding too interested, but she didn't really talk much about it. She took pictures, she said, and when she developed them, I could see for myself.

I remember that that period in my sister's life was hectic for her and even a little hazy and uncertain. She was outwardly excited about starting junior high but reluctant to let go of her comfortable past. It wasn't as if she was afraid because to me, my sister never seemed afraid of anything. It was a happy time for her, but also scarey.

That night, after finding the photo, I asked Mai-Ling how she felt when the photo was taken. She sat and thought for a few minutes, afraid to reveal too much. "I was, well, obviously not happy but determined. Nothing has beat me before and I hope it never will," she explained.

My sister did not repell down that mountain for some thrill or adrenalin rush. Her life before and after that moment has been filled with numerous obstacals she has triumphed over. My sister was born with a cleft pallet. This means she was born without the middle of her top lip, without the right side of her nose, and with a hole in the roof of her mouth. As a highly intelligent child, my sister had a wonderful ear for music. The doctors advised her against swimming, karate, and even playing a musical instrument. When she heard that she couldn't play music, something in her changed because a week later, she came home with a clarinette in her hand.

Mai struggled to learn to play an instrument, but she never quit. She would practice for hours. Her eighth grade year she brought home a baritone saxophone, and by her sophomore year, Mai was a good enough baritone sax player to be in jazz band. I then realized my sister had proved the doctors wrong. It was another accomplishment in her life like the one recorded in the snapshot.

While some people might enlarge or even frame a picture like Mai's to show off, I found this picture thrown in a box pilled under millions of family photos. For most people, repelling down a mountain would be an adventure. for my sister it was just another time in her life when she had to prove to herself that she could do something. I realized that the single snapshot had captured the essence of Mai-Ling's life and who she has become, and I feel proud that she's my sister.

Scoring Model for Narration: Autobiographical Narrative

Score 2

Although the writer has described a sequence of events, this autobiographical narrative's weaknesses outweigh its strengths.

Strong Points:

1. Presents a sequence of events
2. Some variety in sentence structure

Problem Points:

1. Lacks focus and stated purpose for writing
2. Insufficient detail and elaboration
3. Contains no dialogue
4. Lackluster vocabulary
5. Abrupt ending
6. Errors in grammar, punctuation, and spelling

Not So Good School Days

When I first started middle school I was scared, I didn't want to go to a new school and have to meet new people. When I was at Heath Elementary I had two best friends Miranda and Robin, we were all friends with Tara and Lynnette. When we graduated fifth grade we all decided to go to Noah Middle School but during the summer Robin moved to Indiana and Lynnette went to Boone, and Miranda, Tara and me were the only ones who went to Noah.

On the first day of sixth grade I was assigned to a team. Since Noah didn't have no walls each floor is divided up into sections called teams each with a different name. I was on six stars I looked everywhere for Miranda and Tara but, I couldn't find them. Later I found out they were placed on six up which made me more upset that we were not even going to be on the same team.

When I walked into my first class I sat down by myself, then two girls Kimi and Rebecca walked in and sat down with me. They were friendly. We had two classes together, besides English, Math and Science. So after my first day I felt OK about going to Noah.

On my third day of school I was in English talking to my new friends Kimi and Rebecca, a conseler came in and told me I was in the wrong class by mistake, I was not supposed to be in advanst. This is when I learned they put students in different levels. She said I belonged in the Regular class, this made me feel not as smart as the other kids. When I walked in my new class I heard some kids snikering. I decided not to go to school anymore, I missed three days of school. Then Miranda called me to find out why I wasn't at school, I told her about the kids making fun of me. She said come to school on Monday and she would take care of everything. When I showed her the kids that had insulted me. Miranda, Tara and two other girls went up to them. Miranda asked one of the kids what was his problem with me. He began cursing us. We were arguing and insulting each other. A teacher, saw what was happening, and stopped us. All of us got ISAP (in school suspension). It was only the eihth day of school I already had one ISAP.

After that insident no one called me any names or said anything to me for that matter. They stayed away from me, because they were afraid of Miranda.

Scoring Model for Narration: Autobiographical Narrative

Score 1

This writer's attempts to write an autobiographical narrative are unsuccessful.

Problem Points:

1. Not written for specific audience or purpose
2. Confusing sequence of events
3. Few details or elaboration
4. Character and setting not developed
5. No dialogue
6. Confusing sentence patterns
7. Many errors in grammar, punctuation, and spelling
8. Abrupt ending

Playing

I remember starting basketball, it was the best experence I ever had when I was 7. I was in elementry when I started, I was the only girl and the tallest. We had at least only 10 to 12 player. Are mascott was a panther, colors purple and white. We had the best players on the teem, also the best coch that no man or woman could tuch when it come to basketball. Basketball is about teem work when it come to games we did everything as a teem ate together, gos on trips and evin talked about diffrent situtions together. I remember the first game I played at Havrill boys and girls club we played aganst a teem named Truman elementry school brown bears. There school mascott was a brown bear, and there colors were brown and white. They had about 9 players on the team since we were little kids we only needed one refre and sometimes we got a way with braking some rules. Their was this one kid that I knowed for the longest on there teem. Sometimes he didnt want to chek me when we was playing a game because I was a girl plus I was taller and bigger. His name was Bruce Barrett and he was a person that I hung arould with when I was younger. When I play the game it was fun I got to stay in the game the longest I was runnin up and down the basketball court bloking and steeling balls and shooting and making points.

Scoring Model for Narration: Short Story

Score 4

This writer presents a richly detailed short story that includes good character development and convincing dialogue.

Strong Points:

1. Complex presentation of conflict through first-person narrator's point of view
2. Clear, logical sequence of events
3. Abundant details; extraordinary observations and insights
4. Precise word usage
5. Effective, selective use of figurative language
6. Convincing dialogue that furthers the plot
7. Overall fluency
8. Very few mechanical errors

Disappearance

She sits holding the remote, staring at the blank TV screen. Her eyes are clear as water. At least they used to be. As a child, I looked into her eyes and discovered the secrets of life. But for the past year I've seen nothing there. The disease that ravages her brain is like a black hole consuming her personality.

She isn't lost all of the time. She forgets when she's suddenly forced away from her daily routine. In fact, she wasn't really that bad until seven months ago, although she's had Alzheimer's for about five years. She doesn't know she is sick.

"Hey, Grandma," I whisper, hoping she's asleep with her eyes open. Her body shows every one of her eighty-seven years.

She starts, and I hope she'll say one of her nonsense phrases like, "Hoy faloy," followed by a quick, "Can you believe it?" Only I know she won't. She doesn't joke much anymore.

"Who're you?" She questions, like an obstinate warden, her dead eyes boring a hole into me.

"It's me, Grandma. Rory. Wahwee. Remember? I'm your granddaughter. I'm Myra's daughter."

"I can't believe that," she says, turning to face the cream walls. Tiptoeing over to the mahogany bookshelf, I withdraw the rose-red photo album from its place next to my father's medical journals.

"Look, Grandma," I beckon, speaking slowly and opening to the third page, "that's me. See, you're holding me. And look, there's my mom, your daughter, Myra. Remember?"

"Oh, Wahwee!" she chuckles. "There you are! Where am I? This place seems familiar, but I don't know where I am."

I shift my weight from my left to my right foot. Maybe she's just joking. She knows whose house this is. She must.

"Well, Grandma, this is where I live. Myra and Ben's house. You're here with us. Remember?"

"I can't believe that." I feel my stomach caving in on itself; I barely breathe.

"Grandma, it's true."

"This is your house?"

"Yeah, Grandma, it's my mother's and father's. My mother is your daughter. My mother is Myra, and this is her house."

"I have no daughter." Her words are as sharp as a razor blade; not malicious, just unaware.

My eyes fill with tears, and I struggle to blink them away. I love this woman as much as I love anything. She appeared as old and knowing as the moon, and now she's a child again.

"Grandma, there's Myra! See? Look, there she is in the picture!"

"I can't believe that. You're trying to trick me."

I almost turn to leave the room. If I left now she would never know the difference. I wouldn't have to feel this rejection.

"That's my daughter? How do you know?"

"Because Myra is my mother." She looks at me, puzzled, scratching her forehead.

"I think I'm going crazy. I don't know. Maybe. It's vague," she states. A single tear slips out of the corner of my eye, and slithers down my cheek. I brush it away quickly, but she sees.

"Little girl, why do you cry?" I want to tell her then. All I need to say is, "Grandma, you have a disease called Alzheimer's. It makes you forget things." Only it's no use. In five minutes, my words, my face, my life will be erased from her memory.

"Such beautiful black hair," she whispers. My hair is brown, actually, but she loves it and claims that it's black. At least Alzheimer's didn't steal that from me.

"Wait!" She shouts pointing to a photograph of me at a swimming pool, "Is this you here? And there's Myra, my daughter." A smile eats up my face.

"That's right, Grandma. And here you are at my mother's house. See? Who am I?" I drop her palm, and clasp my hands together, shaking them silently. She pauses a moment, then queries,

"Rory, Wahwee?"

"Right!" I exclaim as though the fact that she knows my name is the most fantastic thing in the world; perhaps it is. And everything's fine; it's okay. For that moment, my grandmother has come back from wherever she's been sleeping.

Scoring Model for Narration: Short Story

Score 3

This writer has crafted a short story with basically effective plot development and convincing dialogue.

Strong Points:

1. Effective description of atmosphere
2. Convincing dialogue
3. Good character development
4. Some descriptive detail
5. Predominantly clear sequence of events

Problem Points:

1. Uneven pacing of events
2. Limited use of sensory detail
3. Weak, somewhat rushed story ending

Aftermath

As I stepped out onto the porch the bright sunshine was blinding. A soft breeze swirled around me. I bit into the green apple that had been left out on the kitchen table.

Momma pulled into the driveway. She had light blue eyes, just like mine. Momma loved me like nothing else, and we both knew it. Of course, I loved her too.

"Hey, how was your day?" She always asked. And my usual response was "Fine." She kissed me on the cheek, and I followed her inside the house.

She sighed, "Did you feed the dog today?" One of the few chores that I always seem to forget is feeding Oscar. Even though he greets me when I come home from school, it never crosses my mind that he has to eat. After feeding him, I stepped outside to take him for a walk.

Standing on the street corner with Oscar, I began to feel bothered deep inside the pit of my stomach. My hands started to sweat. I recognized a strange shape in the distance, it appeared to be a gray funnel. Despite being several miles away, it continued to quickly approach me. Items swirled in and around it: a rooftop, a wall, a door, a doghouse, a dog. The earth around me seemed to shake. Dust began to fly in my eyes.

I can be described as one of those people which freeze in the presence of danger. My legs stuck to the ground. I didn't notice Oscar barking his head off. He would growl, bark, then whimper, realizing it was an uneven match for him.

Hearing his barks, Momma came rushing out of the front door. "What is going o . . ." She cut herself off as she spotted me standing in the path of the tornado. She yelled my name. I turned around and ran towards the house. Oscar and I just made it.

We all escaped to the small basement. Where we remained for over an hour. We found an old black radio. Momma searched for weather information.

"The tornado that passed through Tulsa this afternoon has now died down. Now back to the Top Ten at . . ."

Momma, Oscar, and I stepped outside to witness the destruction. Furniture, lost pets, and now homeless people scattered themselves along our street. Cries of pain rang in our ears. A girl from across the street yelled desperately for her mother. She had loved her mother, just as I loved mine. I stared up at Momma. She was watching the girl run around, digging through their house, which the tornado had crushed. Momma stared back at me. She wrapped her arms around my shoulders, and we stood there.

Of course, we were lucky to still have our home, our dog, and most of all, each other. On the other hand, we seemed more than just lucky. The cyclone had missed our house, but came down twice as hard on the others. Guilt filled the pit of my stomach. We gazed at the sights all around us.

Scoring Model for Narration: Short Story

Score 2

Despite this writer's efforts to write an effective short story, its weak points outnumber its strengths.

Strong Points:

1. Clear sequence of events
2. Some good use of sensory detail
3. Clever, unexpected resolution of conflict

Problem Points:

1. Rushed plot development
2. Insufficient elaboration
3. Limited word choice
4. Numerous, distracting grammatical and mechanical errors
5. Run-on sentences

Breakdown

I was driving on Cemetary Road one cloudy evning, heading back to Morganville. I must not of been concentrating on the road and signing too loud to the blaring radio because the next thing I knew I had a flat tire, I pulled to a stop.

I notice I had stopped in front of the cemetary, my first emotion was fright. There I was in front of a graveyard all alone, it could start storming any minute. I set there wondering why, I had got a flat tire in front of a graveyard. The dead people might get me like in the movie "Thriller." I was real worked up, I calmed down and told myself that I did not want to stay there no longer than I all ready had. I got out of my truck to change the tire. When I first opened the door I notice the warm air. As I got the jack out and started to jack my truck up, I had to tell myself that no corpse is going to get me.

I stood up and breathed deep. I looked over the landscape, I could see for miles and miles. There are scattred trees, wheat fields, cows grasing, birds singing, it all made me feel peacefull. The people in the graveyard must be peacefull to. The sun came out from behind the clouds and warmed my skin. These people in the cemetery don't have nothing to worry about. Why would they want to give up this peace to haunt the ungrateful living.

I put all of my tools back where they belonged. As I got into the cab of my truck I smiled. I wasn't scared any more!

Scoring Model for Narration: Short Story

Score 1

This writer's attempt to write an effective short story is unsuccessful.

Problem Points:

1. Missing title
2. Descriptive rather than narrative purpose
3. Insufficient detail and elaboration
4. No character development; no dialogue
5. No significant connections among events
6. Weak vocabulary
7. Repetitious sentence beginnings; poor sentence structures
8. Many mechanical errors; no paragraphs

On the night where the moon was not out I was driving down cemetary road and my pick up died about 1/4 mile beyond cemetary road. It didn't just die it about killed me to because it is a standard. I had music blaring and couldn't hear nothing in the engine, but I knew something was wrong when the tires lock up I put it in newtral got out shaken up, but alright. Then I started the long treck back to town. When I got out I grabbed my coat and worried about my truck because I had a full tank of gas and will have to do some work. Then I heard a noyse in the leaves and forgot about my truck and turned and looked. There wasn't nothing there! Then I took a shortcut over the cemetary and pasturs because it looked like a shorter way to town. I was doing good for a while but, walking through a cemetary at 11:30 with no moon isn't a good idea. I heard a sound and looked, it was a big black bird on top of my grandmas sister's grave. I took off at full speed and was jumping mounds and headstones and then I saw a huge cat, but it wasn't no cat cause it had no tail and it scared me cause of the size! I decided to sit down to get my head strait. Because at that time panick was my worst enemy. I got calmed down then started waking towards the lights. That I hoped was Morganville, America. Then I relized I was walking on a field of somekind I know because there were rows of neatly plowed dirt. I walked on and I was at my grandmas house. I went in and told her what hapened.

Scoring Model for Description

Score 4

This writer presents a creative description that offers rich details and a unified impression of its subject.

Strong Points:

1. Clear, well-elaborated details
2. Strong opening images
3. Logical, effective organization
4. Unified, coherent impression
5. Sensory language
6. No mechanical errors

On Track

Three more races before it's my turn to take the track for my team. The butterflies in my stomach begin to flutter as I commence my usual twenty-second stretches. My legs extend as I pull each ankle up behind me one at a time, and the tense muscles in my firm hamstrings are momentarily relaxed. Without bending my knees, I touch my fingers to my toes to relieve my calves of their tightness. The pungent, icy fragrance of menthol, liberated from the ocean blue Mineral Ice gel being used by all of the girls saturates the tepid air.

I sit quietly. One race is ending and there is only one more before mine. I quickly go to my dad, who is down by the track. He unties and reties my blue and black sprinting shoes with the neon yellow Nike signs on the sides and black rubber sole with small rubber spikes. He does it much better than I would have, pulling just tight enough, tying a double knot, and tucking the laces inside my shoes so I don't trip.

"First call for the 200 meter," says an amplified voice on a megaphone. Oh, my goodness, that's my race! At the first call, I step over to the sign-up table to see if I can reserve myself in my favorite lane, lane 3. Unfortunately, the organizers have already put me in lane 2. Oh, well.

"Second call for the 200 meter." At this call, I start warming up again, jumping up and down quickly and running in place to stretch my legs out once more.

"Last call for the 200 meter." Oh, boy, this is it!

I approach the 200-meter starting line, which is right before the track's second curve. In the background, I hear, "Come on, Elisabeth, you can do it!" The pressure is on! I take off my jacket and throw it in the grass, then walk over to my lane. I set my feet in the metal blocks. My most nervous feeling hits me now. This anticipation is killing me! The person with the starting gun steps up. "Runners take your mark!" I get down and spread my arms out to the topmost corners of the inside of my lane. A million things run through my mind. But I try to keep myself focused. I keep my head down and my body in a static position. "Get set!" I arch my back and bring my head up to face front at the same time. Two seconds of silence go by. Suddenly, BANG! I spring out of the lane, starting with two big steps to get out of the blocks. Immediately I'm rounding the curve, where I gain the lead. I'm thinking of nothing but getting to the finish line as fast as I can. Everybody and everything is blocked out of my senses. I don't hear anything except my own voice in my head and my coach's voice, saying, "Come on, Elisabeth! All the way!"

The finish line is about ten meters away. I push my body to its limit, as my quadriceps begin swerving a little bit. I bend my upper body slightly over the finish line as I pass it, still in running mode.

Exhausted, I run about ten more meters until I come to a slow jog. My teammates are with me now, hugging me and congratulating me. My teammate, who was running the race with me, and I tied for first place. Yes! I'd rather win with a teammate than without her! My breathing is extremely hard and my strained quadriceps are shaking. I raise my arms so I'll breathe easier and shut my eyes for a moment. Very proud of our victory, my teammate and I approach our coach to be greeted with "Great running ladies!" The pressure is over, until the next track meet!

Scoring Model for Description

Score 3

This writer presents a description that is well-organized, highly detailed, and memorable.

Strong Points:

1. Consistent organization
2. Innovative, amusing point of view
3. Abundant, descriptive details
4. Few errors in spelling, punctuation, and grammar

Problem Points:

1. Sensory language appeals only to sense of sight
2. Occasionally diffuse impression of subject
3. Uneven use of elaboration
4. Sentence fragments

One Place to Another

Dear Mom,

Replying to your previous letter, I have found a home for myself past a bunch of leaves, up a flight of stairs, through a tall front door, to the left, down a hall, and through another doorway. Being a room of fairly high stature, I am finding it to be a fairly nice house. I am inhabited by a young boy, Adam Turner by name.

Placed on my right side is a Victorian desk. It once had little labels stuck on, made of removable tape, but now they are strewn around the base.

On top of this desk, there is a rough sheet of protective paper, complete with scribbles, doodles, and math equations galore, overlapping for years (made with the vast sea of pens, pencils, and other tools of artistic intentions).

Across me, on my left side, stands a bed. A bright, silver sheet of fabric hangs from the upper bunk, opaque on the outside, but virtually transparent from the bed.

Ten years of stuffed animals lie past the "ladder" (actually fat, built-in shelves) on the upper bed. They are pulled down when they are needed for any sort of occasion. At the foot of the bed squat large olive green crates, stacked high with knickknacks, marbles, pillows, rainbow cellophane, books, and tissues.

Blocked by the crates is my closet, stuffed and stacked with more bulky green crates from Adam's monthly room cleaning. The twine light string leads to a single, dim light bulb. When pulled, it reveals two sets of shelves, filled with selected "stuffies," as Adam calls them.

The first set holds books. Little scraps of paper once tried to organize them, but they are now in the same condition as the desk labels. The books are thrown about the bookcase, some upright, some sideways, some crammed in so tight you'd need a tool to get them loose. The second set holds items according to shelf. The top shelf holds anything that looks the least bit like a treasure: a chest full of silver dollars, lost teeth, and rolls of money, a Venetian mask box, and Chinese "healthy balls." There are some fuses, paper scraps, and other bits, too. The second shelf houses toys—wire puzzles and flying birds, loose cards, and such. The third shelf is the home of board games. Crammed into the tight space, Adam managed to stuff quite a few games in.

Objects with no other place are positioned on the top of these closet shelves, between the small circus lamp and the CD player. Beside the CD player sits, of course, the CDs. Only classical. Adam can't *stand* to listen to anything but classical. I miss rap music.

In the clothes department, there is this big chest of drawers. The top drawer is used for holding Adam's comic strips, and messes of clothes that have gotten lost on their way to the hooks. At the bottom back of the drawers is a hole, half against the desk, which collects rubber balls and pencils. Quite bothersome for him, I imagine, but entertaining for me.

My floor of me is actually incredibly clean, and, yes, I am much better since my surgery for the glass door. Sorry I didn't write sooner.
Much love,
A. Room

Scoring Model for Description

Score 2

This writer presents a detailed but imprecise description of the subject.

Strong Points:

1. Plentiful details
2. Some sensory language
3. Some focus on creating main impression

Problem Points:

1. Unclear and poorly composed sentences
2. Imprecise use of words
3. Overwrought language and imagery
4. Illogical and inappropriate figurative language
5. Mechanical errors

Sails in the Sunset

The sun sets on her majestical deck, giving her a radiance glow for all to feel admiration. As she begins to dance, her cadance ingulfs her awaiting audience while they gaze in astonishment and appreciation. Her grace and beauty steal the attention from her associates. As she retrieves her passengers, with a quickness she abruptly leaves her admirers breathless and awaiting in anticipation for her next arrival. She then glides down the bay. All around her is serene and comforting, yielding an appealing array of nature from the thunderous waves that create an energetic symphony orchestrated by melodious winds beating at her sails to her aluring, flamboiant colors that pierce the eye with enticement. As she continues to sail down the bay, as hauty and proud as she made her arrival, she gives her guests a view of approaching asthetics.

The entire senerio is nothing short of a natural wonderland. The sky is complete with exotic birds that form a bevy among the deep ocean of the heavens. Their sonorous melodies blend with nature's chorus and fill the sky with pleasant arias. The inhabitants of the water, are in an apparent confluence with one another and seem pleased with the warmth of the blooming sun. All of God's creatures now share their existence and desire to bathe in the sun's warmth. Trees are in full, voluptuous bloom and sway in time with the wind. Together, along with the intense deep waters, they form an exquisit mural of Mother Nature.

Slowly the sun raises highcr to project an ardent beam upon all. From the boat, the whole world seems static as if nothing even matters. All tranquility and peace have become the heart, while encompassing everything. Further in the distant, we now see other boats, as if idly awaiting for her arrival. She smoothly struts down the bay proudly exhibiting her lavish feetures. Her sails boast numerous flags at an aloof height. Her refined body sparkels from the sun's rays. And her sturdy stance guides her with dignity and honor down the bay. Her presence is truly dramatic and overwhelming.

Scoring Model for Description

Score 1

This writer's attempts to present a description are unsuccessful.

Problem Points:

1. Unclear purpose for writing
2. Shifting focus
3. Confusing organization and progression of thoughts
4. Little or no figurative language
5. Little sensory language or details
6. Errors in grammar, punctuation, and spelling
7. Some poor sentence structure

Super Time

The one object from the past that thoghroly shows my family was in the form of a round wooden table. My brothers and I had our own task for preparing the table for the meals. One got the plates, another got the napkens, the last got the eating utensels. This was a rare ocations that I worked together with my brothers. My dad filed the bowls, my mother coked the rest of the meal. Before she finished my brothers and me set at the table wating for the fest. Our mother usally brot the food in large plates and bowls as we set wating. After we started eating, I think how lucky I am in my wunderful family and feel closer to my parents and brothers than any time. Sometimes when I was done with my potatos, I would get secunds even when I was not hungry, so I could set with my family longer. After I was finish, I always thank my mother, so everyone would leave the table and the bond would be broken.

Scoring Model for Persuasion: Persuasive Speech

Score 4

This writer presents a well-reasoned and well-supported persuasive speech.

Strong Points:

1. Opening paragraph attracts audience's interest and concern
2. Clear statement of position and focus on persuasive task
3. Specific, well-elaborated reasons that provide convincing support for the speaker's position
4. Clear, consistent organizational strategy
5. Many transitions incorporated for clarity
6. Strong, concise, persuasive words
7. Closing that reinforces argument by making an appeal for action
8. Few or no mechanical errors

Plea for Forests

Fellow Inhabitants of Earth:

I invite you all to join me in the depths of the forest. It's a normal, carefree day in the forest. The birds are singing and all of the animals are calm and relaxed, going about their daily business under the refreshing glow of the sun. But suddenly, the thunderous sound of a chain saw echoes throughout the woodlands and trees fall violently. The creatures of the forest run in terror. Many of these beautiful creatures will starve to death slowly and painfully as their homes are destroyed and their food carried away by the men who quickly chop and burn this ecosystem, which will not be able to regrow to its previous greatness for many years to come.

This sad story is a true one in many places around the globe. We must slow deforestation and replant trees immediately to save our breathable air, fertile topsoil, and beautiful organisms.

If entire forests continue to be obliterated less oxygen will be produced and more CO_2 eliminated. In fact, deforestation accounts for a quarter of the CO_2 released into the atmosphere each year: about 1–2 billion tons each year. Forests provide the majority of the oxygen on Earth, and if these forests disappear our air will soon be unbreathable. Future generations will choke on the very air they breathe as easily as a person might choke on a 6-inch wide piece of steak. Without clean air, this planet is uninhabitable for humans and countless innocent animals.

Second, deforestation results in a loss of topsoil. Many of the companies who are involved in deforestation claim that the land is needed for farms, but deforestation makes the land much less fertile than it would be if small sections were required in the future. According to the UN Food and Agriculture Organization, deforestation has damaged almost 6 million sq. km. of soil. Forests are some of the most fertile lands on Earth, but this topsoil can only be used through slow and careful planning, not quick cutting and burning.

Finally, if cutting doesn't slow, many species will die off and many ecosystems will be destroyed. The 2000 UN Global Environment Outlook says that forests and rain forests have the most diverse plants and animals in the world. The GEO also notes that there are more than 1000 threatened species living in the forests of the world. It is a crime to kill entire plant and animal species in the selfish act of destroying forests, yet this crime is committed very often throughout the world. Imagine how it would be if someone came and destroyed all of the houses in your neighborhood. All of the residents would be left homeless, and many would die. This is how it is for the organisms that live in the forests.

In conclusion, deforestation must slow and trees must be replanted immediately, or we will lose clean air, topsoil, and many beautiful organisms. Furthermore, a loss in forests will result in a generation that knows very little about nature. So, to prevent the chaotic disturbance of peace in the forests, please do whatever you can to prevent deforestation and vote yes on any UN bills that would help the condition of our world's forests. Thank you all.

Scoring Model for Persuasion: Persuasive Speech

Score 3

This writer presents a persuasive speech that is supported with reasons and examples.

Strong Points:

1. Stated focus on persuasive task
2. Generally effective word choice
3. Fair organizational strategy
4. Reasons and examples that support persuasive position

Problem Points:

1. Some errors of grammar, word usage, and punctuation
2. Minor instances of faulty logic; disgression
3. Mixed and inappropriate figurative language

Give Us Music

Members of the School Board:

I come here today, to express my feelings on the cutting of musical programs in our schools. When a budget cut needs to be made, music and art programs are the first to go. This is a big mistake, because of the influence that music has on a lot of people's lives, especially mine.

When I hear a song my chest rises and fills with joy. I sit back, and let the musical notes cover my body and take me to a world that is unknown. A world where nothing matters and everything is at peace. There is no one there but me and the warm soulful voice of D'Angelo or the gentle plucking on "Lucille" as B. B. King's husky voice tells the tale of the deep south. I become one with the music. Its like a piece of me that was lost and now is found.

Music is my life. When I wake up, in the mornings I hear the slow, mellow tunes of the radio. And at night, I am rocked to sleep in an ocean of love songs. It has taken me a long time to fully understand the power that musicians possess. They have the power to make a person cry, laugh, and become angry all in a three minute song. Musicians hold the key to peoples hearts.

Although I tend to find my outlet in rap and R&B music, I can also listen to classical music and jazz and find the same things. When I was younger, my friends would tease me and call me old or say that I was a sellout because the type of music that I liked consisted of more than rap. While my friends were out listening to Will Smith and Kool Moe D, I sat at my mother's feet and listened to Billie Holiday and Nat King Cole. But soon my mother began to push me into the world saying, "You are too young, why don't you go and play with your friends." And with that, my world of music was lost. I never wanted to be so narrow minded, and just like one type of music and nothing else.

My eight grade year, I walked into my music class and was slapped in the face by the sounds of African drums. I took my seat and found myself rocking backwards and forwards to the beat. I had found what I thought was forever lost to me, a different kind of music. Each day when I went into my music class, I was greeted with a new type of music that I had lost.

My music teacher told me that my love of music was never lost and that it just needed that extra push to be able to shine. Ever since that day in music class when the magical world of music was unleashed to me I have grabbed it up and ran with it. I listen to alternative, jazz, classical, rock and roll, R&B and even rap.

I think that music is a good outlet and should be used by all. I want people to know that inside each of them is a small box that is waiting to be unlocked and set free. People need to expand their minds and let the music take over and glide them into an unknown world.

In closing I would like to say that I am not the only person who feels this way about music. I have seen music classes bring out parts of people that no one even knew were there. It would be a shame to pull out music programs because it limits the minds of students. I am asking please try to find a way to keep music in schools because it is really needed.

Scoring Model for Persuasion: Persuasive Speech

Score 2

Although this writer has attempted to state a persuasive position, the weaknesses of the persuasive speech outweigh its strengths.

Strong Points:

1. Some persuasive reasons provided
2. Some details that support ideas

Problem Points:

1. Inconsistent organizational strategy
2. Several examples of faulty logic or unclear reasoning
3. Few transitions
4. Weak links between some ideas
5. Irrelevant information
6. Errors of grammar, spelling, and punctuation

Texas Comemorative Quarter

Honorable Members of the State Legislature:

What feetures exist as Texas' most distingished and recognizible ones. One that fits is the akual outline of Texas. I understand you must aprove of any suggestions on the design of the Texas comemerative quarter so I am proposing one that holds meaning in the hearts of Texans and would also be educational for all the people. A important characteristics of Texas is its akual outline, therefore, children all over the United States tend to recognize it. Texas distinguishes itself through its outline and because the United States Mint has decided the comemerative quarters must for education, I strongly recommend that we use the outline of Texas in the quarter.

The shape of Texas does not resemble a square or box like other states which shows that Texas varys from other states. Texas fought Mexico over the south bourder to keep it as the Rio Grand when they could have just surendered to Mexico's claims, which would have placed the bourder further inland. The decision to go into battle was decided even where in comparison to the rest of Texas, the akual land which we would have lost proved to be of basically unimportant proportions.

Another reason Texas' outline should reside on the comemerative quarter relates to the fact that the coin could then be compared to other state shapes. Texas remains the second largest state in America, and that should be evident in the eyes of the children. When kids see the states outline on a coin they ought to recall learning that Texas is a massive state and that should trigger how Texas become so big. After all, the old saying states, "The bigger, the better."

I believe other symbols should be placed on it as well. Our state motto "the friendly state" could be at the top of the state, while the state bird and flower shold remain on each side of the quarter.

Thank you for taking the time to listen to my sugestions on the design of the comemerative quarter and I hope you choose to use it for the Texas quarter.

Scoring Model for Persuasion: Persuasive Speech

Score 1

Although this writer's work does express a persuasive purpose, it fails to be a persuasive speech.

Problem Points:

1. Weak opening and closing position statements
2. Confusing presentation
3. Little attention to the audience
4. Awkward sentence construction
5. Digression from main points
6. Many grammatical errors
7. Poor word usage, including vague referents

Sports Programs in the Schools

Ladies and Gentlemen:

It has been brout to my atention that some peoples think that schools place to much importance on sports. I strongly disagree with this issue because sports is healthy, players represent our school and most important it keeps students away from getting into trouble.

The most important thing in life is being healthy. It is the important key for living longer and not having no health problems, by this I mean that sports keeps students with no time for doing lazy stuff like eating and tv all day. In a magazine they said where everyone have to be active by playing sports and stop eating to much. So quit being lazy and start playing a sport, for example football is 80% mental and 20% physical, so it is not all physical, it can be educational. Players show how grate our school is by playing sports. A team is very important in life because every where you go you see teams. Sports need a lot of practice and take a lot of time which causes students from being out on the streets. Last night on t.v. they said where students that didn't take sports ended up in the wrong way of life. In conclusion sports does help most students. It's like the saying goes "it is better to prevent it than from regreting it." I would really like you take my reasons in considerasion

Scoring Model for Persuasion: Advertisement

Score 4

This writer combines language and design elements to create a strongly persuasive advertisement.

Strong Points:

1. Logical organization
2. Effective persuasive strategy
3. Graphic elements that support persuasive purpose
4. Effective use of language
5. Very few mechanical errors

Do you know someone who can't read?

You can help.
On Saturday, May 27, 2000, two authors will be in town
to help raise funds for the Eastham Reading Council's Literacy Fund.

Verna McPherson, author of *Folkloric*,
and
**Lise Montgomery,
author of *The Life and Lore of Angela Gordon*,**

will sign copies of their books at Basement Books in Eastham Mall.
This event is free of charge and will be held from 10 A.M.
until 12:45 P.M. Twenty-five percent of the proceeds from
each book purchase will go to the Literacy Fund.

You'll have a second chance to hear and meet the
authors at 8 P.M. at the Eastham Public Library.
They will present a discussion of folklore and literacy.
All who attend the library presentation will receive a
20 percent discount coupon for Angela Gordon titles at Basement Books.
Don't miss this folkloric fund-raiser.
The people you help may be people you know!
For more information, call 555-2124

Scoring Model for Persuasion: Advertisement

Score 3

This writer has combined verbal and visual elements to create a fairly persuasive advertisement.

Strong Points:

1. Interest-grabbing slogan
2. Layout and design elements convey generally effective organizational strategy
3. Words and images cooperate to support persuasive position
4. Adequate use of language

Problem Points:

1. Some information presented out of sequence
2. A few mechanical errors

Extra! Extra! Read all about it!

Saturday, May 27, 2000 two important events will take place.

Ms. Verna McPherson, author of *Folkloric*,
and
Ms. Lise Montgomery, award winning author of
***The Life and Lore of Angela Gordon*,**

will present a dialogue on "American Folklore."
This discussion, followed by a book signing, will be held
in the auditoreum of the Eastham Public Library.
If you are unable to attend the 8:00 P.M. discussion,
Ms. McPherson and Ms. Montgomery will be signing books
at Basement Books between 10:00 A.M. and 12:45 P.M.
Both events are free. Twenty-five percent of the
purchase price of the author's books will be
donated to the local Books for Non-Readers Fund
of the Eastham Reading Council. Attendents will
receive a 20 percent discount coupon good at
Basement Books for the purchase of any book by Angela Gordon.

The Eastham Public Library is located at the intersction of Victoria Blvd. and McKenzie Rd.
Basement Books is located in the Eastham Mall near Josephine's Apparel Shop.

Scoring Model for Persuasion: Advertisement

Score 2

While this writer has presented basic information necessary for an advertisement, the weaknesses of the advertisement outnumber its strengths.

Problem Points:

1. Slogan lacks originality
2. Incomplete or misplaced information
3. Does not persuade by motivating reader to attend event
4. Language not used to enhance persuasive effect
5. Elements of layout and design lack visual appeal and persuasive strategy
6. Many mechanical errors

Don't miss it

The program "American Folklore"
is holding a book sining at the Eastham Mall
inside Basement books. It will be Held on Saturday—
May 27, 2000.
Sinings 10:00 AM. to 12:45 P.M.
Then the writers will be speaking at the
Eastham public library at 8: PM.
The Library is at the intersection of
Victoria Blvd. And McKenzie Rd. in
Eastham 20 percent coupon good at
Basement Books by Angela Gordon for attending.
25 percent of the purchase price of
each authors' book will be donaited to
the Eastham Reading Concil Books for non readers Fund.

Scoring Model for Persuasion: Advertisement

Score 1

This writer's efforts to produce a persuasive advertisement are unsuccessful.

Problem Points:

1. Lacks slogan
2. Lacks purposeful design concept
3. Little attention to persuasive task
4. Weak organizational strategy
5. Confusing presentation of information; some information missing
6. Unclear explanation of persuasive offer
7. Poor use of language
8. Numerous mechanical errors

A book sining at Basement Books in Eastham Mall (located near the Josephine's Apparel Shop). The two authors that will be there Verna McPherson and Lise Montgomery. The sining will take place 10:00 A.M. until 12:45 P.M. Also a program at the Eastham Public Library "American Folklore" that will be at 8:00 P.M.

Any person that intrested in the folklore of Angela Gordon should atend both. Each atendant will recieve a 20% off her books coupon.

Scoring Model for Exposition: Comparison-and-Contrast Essay

Score 4

This writer presents a strong comparison-and-contrast essay with consistent organization.

Strong Points:

1. Reason stated for comparison-and-contrast analysis
2. Well-constructed introductory paragraph
3. All information linked to comparison-and-contrast premise
4. Consistent organization suited to the topic
5. Elaboration of ideas with details and examples
6. Variety of sentence structures
7. Strong vocabulary
8. Few mechanical errors

Fundamentally, Equals

When the powers of good and evil collide, a battle is inevitable. At first glance, Graham Green's *The Power and the Glory* appears to agree with this idea. However, under closer observation of the two great adversaries in the novel, the whiskey-priest and the lieutenant, it would be difficult to say clearly who is good and who is evil. Graham Greene tends to take the sides of both characters, creating an interesting conflict. In an initial comparison, the two seem to be opposites—the whiskey-priest playing the criminal and the lieutenant playing the cop. But is the criminal bad and the cop good? Or are both good and both bad? When both personalities are examined, their equality becomes clear.

The main character, the whiskey-priest is a paradox. Being a holy man, he is obliged to serve the poor and defenseless and to put others before himself. On the other hand, "whiskey" implies something altogether unholy. Drunkenness was one of his great sins, and he openly admitted it. Time after time, he cursed his weakness for drink. He does, however, ask for forgiveness for his drunkenness at the end when he confesses his sins.

Another fascinating aspect of the whiskey-priest's personality is his willingness to pray for others and his forgiving nature. In that aspect, the whiskey-priest fulfills his duties as a holy father when he says to the half-caste who betrayed him, "I'll pray for you." (p. 197) In the end, he even prayed for the lieutenant, the man who brought him to his death. He repeatedly forgives and prays for those whose paths he crosses.

Despite the whiskey-priest's strong devotion to God, he also displays extremely low self-esteem. When talking with the lieutenant he states, "But I'm not a saint. I'm not even a brave man." (p. 195) The whiskey-priest is persistent in his belief that he has sinned too greatly against God to be anything more than a drunk.

Lastly, the whiskey-priest shows mixed emotions about his want and fear of death. Many times he wants it all to be over soon. Yet he believes that he is one of the last true priests. In the end, he walked openly into what he knew was a trap. This final act of sacrifice dissolves the conflicts of want and fear of death.

On the other end of the personality spectrum lies the lieutenant. At first, the lieutenant may appear to be the whiskey-priest's enemy or rival, but exploring his personality suggests otherwise. First, although the lieutenant does not believe in the church, he is very open-minded. He is willing to listen to the whiskey-priest and have long discussions with him about God and the church. The lieutenant replies to one of the whiskey-priest's inquiries saying, "I am not afraid of other people's ideas." (p. 197)

Even though the lieutenant sticks by his beliefs, he exhibits excellent insight and thought into the topic of God and the church. Surprisingly, at the end, the lieutenant summons Padre José so the priest may confess all his sins and be forgiven. The lieutenant risks imprisonment, but he does so because he knows it is important for the whiskey-priest's beliefs.

The Lieutenant reveals a kind heart and warm, loving nature underneath his rough exterior. When the priest was a prisoner in jail, the lieutenant took pity on him. The lieutenant, breaking the anti-liquor law demonstrated his kindness when he gave the whiskey-priest brandy on his last night in prison.

The lieutenant shows clear confusion in his thinking. He believes, basically, that priests are sinful creatures of a false God. He loves the poor people of the villages dearly and believes that the priests do no good for them. It is odd that the lieutenant has a prejudice against priests yet is a loving man. Like the whiskey-priest, the lieutenant is a paradox. He is polite and civil one moment, yet a heartless tyrant at another.

In conclusion, both the whiskey-priest and the lieutenant display characteristics of traditional good and evil. Neither is all good nor all bad in the extreme.

Scoring Model for Exposition: Comparison-and-Contrast Essay

Score 3

This writer presents a fairly effective comparison-and-contrast essay.

Strong Points:

1. Reason stated for comparison-and-contrast analysis
2. Organization suited to the topic
3. Elaboration with ideas and examples
4. Good sentence variety and vocabulary

Problem Points:

1. No introductory paragraph; title and author not identified
2. Too few direct quotes
3. Some mechanical errors
4. Weak concluding paragraph

Good and Bad

Though there are many ideas that seperate the priest and the lieutenant, there is no distinguishing thought that makes one man good and one man evil.

The priest is good because he is trying to help people and spread the word of God. However, the priest has many faults that contradict his role as a priest, therefore he cannot be classified as good. The lieutenant would be bad since he is pursuing the priest, yet so many good qualities shine through the lieutenant's personality that he can't be called bad. The differences between the whiskey priest and the lieutenant are what make them interesting subjects to compare and contrast.

It is assumed that the priest is a good person. But that is not true as his nickname "the whiskey priest" suggests. The priest has many faults, and the most prodominate fault is that he drinks too much. At one point he was drunk and baptized a little boy with the name Brigitta instead of Pedro.

Although the priest has many sins, he cannot be condemned. The priest also has some good traits. He is willing to administer the last rites, give masses, and say prayers. The priest befriends a lot of people in his journey. For those reasons, it is difficult to decide whether or not he is the good guy.

In the end, the priest finally begins to truly change. "He felt like someone who has missed happiness by seconds at an appointed place. He knew that at the end there was only one thing that counted—to be a saint." (p. 210) What he had come to realize was how wrong his sins were, and how because of his mistakes he couldn't become the only thing that mattered—to be a saint. His thought shows how he has changed and brings out the goodness in him.

The lieutenant is the one who seems as though he should be bad. He is pursuing the priest, but he is only following his duty. The lieutenant is also good in some ways. He gives 5 pesos to the priest to help him, and he even brings the priest some brandy near the end. The lieutenant attempts to get Padre José to come and let the priest confess to him. Therefore, everything bad he does is contradicted by something good.

As the priest and the lieutenant come from seperate worlds, they do share one thing, the act of running away and pursuing. The priest is running away from the lieutenant, yet he is also running from his sins, from his drinking, and from himself. Yet he is pursuing religion, trying to gain it back. The lieutenant is running from religion and from his childhood in which he had a bad time with religion. The two characters also share a deep devotion to their jobs. They both put a lot of effort into their jobs, not just for themselves. The priest does it for the people and to keep religion alive. The lieutenant does it for the governor and to get better childhoods for the children.

Overall, it appears that the priest and the lieutenant had very different views and opinions, yet both of them shared such passion for religion. The lieutenant was against it, and the priest was for it, yet because of it they were brought together. So, they're never seperated as good and evil, but their weaknesses and strengths are now known.

Scoring Model for Exposition: Comparison-and-Contrast Essay

Score 2

Although this writer has attempted to organize and support ideas appropriate to a comparison-and-contrast essay, the essay's weaknesses are more numerous than its strengths.

Strong Points:

1. Identifies some points for comparison and contrast
2. Some effort at effective organization for comparison and contrast

Problem Points:

1. Unclear thesis statement; title and author not identified
2. Disorganized ideas and details
3. First-person narration inconsistent with analysis
4. Insufficient elaboration to support generalizations
5. Errors of mechanics, usage, and spelling

The Priest and Luetenant

"You're a good man. You've got nothing to be afraid of" says the priest.

I chose to open my paper with this statement because this opening shows the vast difference between the Priest and Luetenant. The two differances between the Priest and Luetenant that are evident are fear and morale.

The Priest was a fearful man. He was scared of being caught and dying. He was also afraid of being alone. He uses brandy to ease all his fears and take the pain away.

The Luetenant doesn't ever seem to be afraid. He always holds his head up high. He's determined, and that is what makes him oblivious to the fear of erasing Priests and robbers. The determination comes from a well inside of him that wants to make the world a better place for the children. This brings me to my second point.

In the novel both men are good and evil in their own ways. The Priest is evil in the all the sins he has comited and all the times he's fallen short. The Priest is a good man for trying to stay alive and continuing masses even after he knew the police were persuing him.

The luetenant is evil for wanting to take the church away from the children. The Luetenant was a good man because he thought he was doing what he thought best. He also showed the Priest compasion on some ocasions like getting him a priest for confesion.

The two men are differant in many other ways also. One of these is strong in morals and the other is supposed to be. They are both dissapointed in theirselves.

In this paper I have explored many ideas as to how the Luetenent and Priest are alike and how they aren't. As you can see, there are more differances than similarities but, they are there.

Scoring Model for Exposition: Comparison-and-Contrast Essay

Score 1

This writer's attempt to write a comparison-and-contrast essay is unsuccessful.

Problem Points:

1. Lacks reason for comparison-and-contrast analysis
2. Lacks effective organization and structure for comparison-and-contrast
3. Lacks understanding of comparison-and-contrast exposition
4. Insufficient facts and examples to support main ideas
5. Poor use of language; run-on sentences; no paragraphs
6. Many mechanical errors

Leutenant vs. Priest

In the areas of religion and integrity, the priest and the litenant are very different. For instance the priest beleaves in religion while the lieitenant could care less. The priest is a relegious man where the leutenant is a buisnesmen. The priest is trying to spread religion and the lietenant is trying to kill off all the priests. Both of these men do things that hurt other people but they still feel for them. In the area of integrety I believe that they both have low integrety because they dont care about anyone other than their selves. The priest says he is a holy man because he gives mass to the villagers and then he goes out and gets drunk. The leutenant give the priest a five-cent piece. Which was co-insidently the price of the wine needed for a mass. He also comforts the priest. During his last hours. With these examples, I believe that these men are seen wrong even though portrayed as dishonorable men, the priest and the leutenant both have truly good hearts.

Scoring Model for Exposition: Cause-and-Effect Essay

Score 4

This writer presents a clear, well-elaborated cause-and-effect essay with a consistent organizational strategy and effective examples.

Strong Points:

1. Thesis statement clearly identifies audience and purpose
2. Clear, logical organizational strategy
3. Successfully linked causes and effects
4. Transitions between paragraphs create a unified essay
5. Varied sentence structure
6. Effective conclusion
7. Precise word usage; excellent vocabulary
8. No mechanical errors

Factors Contributing to School Violence

According to *Webster's Dictionary*, violence is defined as "physical force used so as to injure, damage, or destroy" or "the unjust or callous use of force or power as in violating another's rights, sensibilities, etc." Under this definition, fist-fighting, name-calling, vandalism, and property theft can all qualify as acts of violence, since each of these acts violates a person's rights. These acts are typically the forms of violence experienced by students in school. The causes of such acts of violence may be as varied as the students who commit them. However, according to news reports and articles on the subject, there appear to be three significant factors that may serve as catalysts for violence: a tumultuous family history, peer group rejection, and inability to deal with anger or aggression. All these factors may play a role in the increased incidence of school violence.

Emotional and combative family disputes in a student's home may lead to violent school behavior on the part of that student. Family issues, such as an unstable child-parent relationship, can place serious emotional burdens on the student. For example, if the student has argued with a parent about rights or responsibilities in the morning before school begins, that student may arrive at school in a combative mood. As a result, the student may initiate arguments or engage in otherwise destructive behavior. Disruptions in the student's home life, therefore, may result in disruptions at school.

Students may also engage in violent behavior because of rejection by their peers. Such rejection may cause the students to take out their frustrations in violent acts. For instance, a student who is friendless because he or she dresses differently from other students in school may feel angry and resentful about the negative treatment and may expressed these feelings through physical violence. Violence may be the student's means of attaining revenge or it may bolster his or her self-esteem to physically assert superiority over a younger or weaker student. Thus, destructive peer relationships may increase the level of violence in schools.

The idea that students who are rejected by their peer groups may turn to violence to alleviate their anger and frustration relates to a final possible cause for the increase in school violence: bullying. The aggressive nature of school bullies also contributes to the increased number of violent school incidents. Bullies emotionally and physically taunt weaker, less aggressive students to bolster their own low self-esteem. As a result, bullies are also a major factor in why school violence has increased in recent years.

Each of these factors that cause school violence—a difficult family life, peer rejection, and school bullies—has its basis in a student's inability to deal with a difficult situation without resorting to violence. In many cases, schools can change the violent behavior of their students by making a serious investment in time and resources. Counseling programs, in which students can speak to professional therapists, may enable students to learn how to cope in a nonviolent way. Students may also benefit from participating in peer meditation groups, where other students trained in peaceful mediation techniques can help to defuse a tense situation. In addition, presentations by professionals in the field of psychology or sociology may provide a valuable source of information for students and teachers in coping with violent school incidents. Finally, in extreme cases, it may be an option to find an alternative means of educating severely disruptive students.

Whatever method school officials choose to implement in order to reduce the number of violent episodes in school, it is important for them to keep in mind why students are violent in order to determine how to stop this destructive and sometimes tragic behavior.

Scoring Model for Exposition: Cause-and-Effect Essay

Score 3

This writer presents a well-organized and focused cause-and-effect essay.

Strong Points:

1. Well-written introduction with good lead and clearly stated purpose for writing
2. Clear organizational strategy
3. Clearly linked causes and effects
4. Good conclusion

Problem Points:

1. Lacks full elaboration and specific examples
2. Run-on sentences and fragments
3. Minor mechanical errors

Analyzing the Reasons

In the wake of serious incidents of school violence in Colorado, Arkansas, and Kentucky, many people have begun to analyze the reasons for such terrible outbursts in order to develop methods to prevent them from ever happening again. There are a wide variety of reasons to explain why students behave violently. But three reasons include dissatisfaction with one's peer group, jealousy or rivalry with school peers, or problems at home. Any of these factors can lead to a violence episode at school.

Sometimes, teens feel isolated from and rejected by other students in their grade or class, this isolation may arise because the rejected teen looks, acts, or speaks differently then the majority of the students. While the teen does feel hurt by the rejection of the other students, this hurt can turn to resentment and anger. When the resentment and anger becomes too much to handle, the teenager may translate it into a violent act. Like fighting.

An inability to deal with feelings of intense jealousy of another student at school. Whether it is over sports, academics, or personal issues like appearance, may also be a source of increased school violence. A student can feel insecure about his or her own abilities and appearance and jealousy can channel these insecurities onto a specific person who seems to be superior. When the jealous student can no longer handle these strong feelings, he or she may start a fight with the student who is the object of the jealousy. In an effort to get rid of them.

Finally, many teenagers bring their family problems to school in the form of disrespectful or agressive behavior. Such difficult home experiences like continuous arguments or destructive behavior take an emotional toll on the teen, the teen also does not have a good role model of positive ways to interact with people in difficult situations. As a result, when the teen is faced with a difficult situation in school, he or she will argue or fight rather than find a way to resolve the situation peacefully.

As you can see, school violence is a complicated issue, which can occur for a variety of reasons. Peer rejection, jealousy, and family difficulties are only three sources for school violence. Although knowing the sources of school violence can help school officials to develop methods to prevent it. Since these three cause of school violence have a basis in emotional issues, school officials may want to consider developing a special counceling program as a way to help students to cope with their violence feelings in a positive way. Perhaps in this way, school violence can be reduced.

Scoring Model for Exposition: Cause-and-Effect Essay

Score 2

Although this writer presents an organized cause-and-effect essay, its weaknesses outweigh its strengths.

Strong Points:

1. Logical organization
2. Some valid cause-and-effect analysis

Problem Points:

1. No clear purpose or thesis statement
2. Lacks elaboration on ideas and specific examples
3. Weak conclusion
4. Run-on sentences and fragments
5. Numerous mechanical errors

Causes of School Violence

In the past several years, there have violent incidents in schools all over the country. School violence has increased for different reasons. Some not even related to school. Unhappiness with a peer group, school achievement, or home life are the reasons.

For many students, how happy they are in school depends on if they have lots of friends. If they feel like they are popular, they feel good about themselfs and they don't make trouble. But if a student feels like an outcast and no one really likes them, that students resentment can grow until it becomes a violent episod.

School achievement can also lead to violent behavior. When a student does poorly in school, that student may take out there frustrations by fighting with other students.

Last, although it is not directly related to events in school, a hard home life can lead to trouble at school. Arguments between parents and children can turn into arguments and fights at school. They take thier anger that they are not alowed to show at there parents out on people at school.

We need to do something about school violence one thing we can do is help kids by giving them counseling about how to deal with their problems, maybe then there will be a decrease of violence in schools.

Scoring Model for Exposition: Cause-and-Effect Essay

Score 1

This writer's efforts to write an effective cause-and-effect essay are unsuccessful.

Problem Points:

1. No clear purpose for writing
2. No specific target audience
3. Lacks organizational strategy
4. Insufficient exposition of connections between causes and effects
5. Lacks a conclusion
6. Many errors in sentence structure and mechanics

School Violence

School violence has increased for many reasons such as, a ruff time at home, bullying, and being jelous of people.

One reasons why there is more school violence in school is because the student who come to school have a roiugh home life. They and there parents rgue a lot. The student come to school still angry over the fight with them. Another reason, there is more school violence is because there is bullies who pick on weaker student. When the weak student fight back more violence hapens. The last reason for school violence is jelousy. One student is jelous of another clothes, jewelry, etc, and they fights over it, like to prove who is better. So these is the reasons there is violence in school.

Scoring Model for Exposition: Problem-Solution Essay

Score 4

This writer has written a strong problem-solution essay.

Strong Points:

1. Clear definition of problem and identification of solutions
2. Effective organization
3. Full elaboration of main ideas
4. Style well suited to subject
5. Engaging use of details
6. Sound mechanics, with few errors

A Cure

What is singultus, and how can you cure it? Singultus is the phenomenon we usually call the hiccups. Hiccups are common, and almost everyone experiences them from time to time. Yet despite the familiarity of hiccups, experts are uncertain about what exactly causes the condition and how to cure it. Perhaps because the reasons remain mysterious, home remedies for the hiccups flourish. Some sound far-fetched, yet often work; other remedies seem reasonable, but fail to solve the problem. Here is an exploration of hiccups and their cure.

A hiccup is basically an involuntary spasm of the diaphragm. The diaphragm is the muscle located at the base of the ribs right below the lungs. Its purpose is to help control one's breathing patterns. When the diaphragm has a spasm, air rushes to the lungs causing the glottis, a gap between the vocal cords, to close. This causes the air to get caught and squeezed in the vocal cords, which is what makes the "hiccup" sound. Hiccups will continue until the spasms in the diaphragm stop.

What causes the spasms in the diaphragm to occur? One thing that can cause it is a nerve impulse from the part of one's brain that controls the breathing. The pattern is then disturbed, thus causing the spasm in the diaphragm. The second thing that can cause it is an imprecise message sent by the phrenic nerves from the neck area of the spinal cord. These nerves regulate the diaphragm, and when disturbed may cause spasms. Other things that may trigger hiccups are big meals or drinking too much alcohol, or they may occur as a secondary complication to a disease like pneumonia or diabetes. Eating too much hot, cold, or spicy food, eating too fast, and gulping air could lead to hiccups. In some people, nervousness can bring on bouts of hiccups by allowing abnormal impulses to be set off in the part of the brain that controls the breathing pattern. If that happens, calming your breathing patterns back down to normal could make hiccups less likely.

What can be done to cure this strange phenomenon? Most often hiccups will go away on their own. Of course, there are many home remedies to try. Remedies that stimulate the gag reflex usually work best. Increasing the carbon dioxide in the blood by breathing in and out of a paper bag could help. Here are some other home remedies: eat a spoon full of white or brown sugar; drink a glass of water upside down; put your hands over your ears, drink a glass of water while holding your breath; or simply hold your breath as long as you can. According to home remedies, you can also be scared out of the hiccups. My personal favorite is to "tickle" the top of the mouth with one's tongue. If the hiccups are prolonged, prescribed medication like baclofen and chlorpromazine can be taken to cure them.

In conclusion, hiccups may be annoying and inconvenient but they cause no harm to your health and are usually over quickly. Even though doctors are not certain why the diaphragm has these spontaneous spasms, we do know the chain reaction that causes the hiccups. To solve the hiccup problem, there are many home remedies and some prescription medications that can relieve hiccups.

Scoring Model for Exposition: Problem-Solution Essay

Score 3

This writer presents a well-reasoned problem-solution essay.

Strong Points:

1. Appropriate language and details for the subject
2. Clear, logical organization
3. Well-identified problem
4. Clearly elaborated solution

Problem Points:

1. Occasional poor sentence structure
2. Limited word choice; faulty usage
3. Mechanical errors

Strict Restrictions

In 1995, 2,000,000 automobile accidents occurred in the age group of 16–18. Five hundred sixty-nine thousand teenagers died in these automobile accidents. These statistics lead me to believe that teenage drivers between the ages of 16 and 18 should have restrictions placed on them when they get their licenses.

Restricted licenses should only be the kind issued to those between the ages of 16 and 18. Restrictions imposed should include limits to driving only during daylight hours, no one under the age of 18 allowed in the car with the driver, no use of cell phones while driving, and no driving out of town without written consent. Many accidents happen at night due to impaired vision, showing off, driving while drinking, speeding, and also because of simply misjudging curbs, turns, and traffic lights. Having another teenager under the age of 18 in the car leads to a greater chance of being distracted, as the driver is usually paying more attention to his friends than driving. A cell phone works the exact same way. The driver, usually driving with one hand, concentrates more on the phone than on his driving. Those caught driving out of town will have their license taken away and be fined $500.00–$5,000.00, depending on why they were pulled over.

Once the restricted license has been obtained, the driver will have to renew it every six months, and also thereby allowing their driving record to be checked for tickets or accidents. If the driving record is clean for a year extra driving privileges will be added.

The reason for the renewing of the license every six months instead of after a year will make teenage drivers more conscious of their driving. Those who choose to be immature while driving and get into an accident or get a speeding ticket are to have their license taken away immediately. Thereby preventing another accident waiting to happen. Also if the driver attends school on a regular basis and is passing all of his courses, they will receive extra privileges. These privileges may consist of an extra hour or two of driving after the sun has gone down, having a friend ride along, or being allowed to drive out of town without written consent. All these are steps toward full privileges, which should be given only if teens maintain a clean record.

Many states have already begun such programs, giving restricted licenses to teenage drivers, although these are state laws, I hope that one day they will become federal law. Five hundred sixty-nine thousand teenagers died in 1995 and the number just gets higher each year. Restricted driving for teenagers is the best solution to this devastating problem.

Scoring Model for Exposition: Problem-Solution Essay

Score 2

This writer includes some inconsistencies in the problem-solution essay and fails to elaborate fully upon the solution.

Strong Points:

1. Statement of the problem to be solved
2. Most language and details suitable to audience
3. Fair word choice and sentence variety

Problem Points:

1. Some details detract from purpose
2. Some unclear or faulty logic
3. Organizational inconsistencies
4. Insufficient elaboration upon solution
5. Errors of grammar, spelling, and punctuation

A Proposed Solution

Dear Folks,

I've been thinking long and hard about what you told me, I owe you an apology. My grades have been bad, I'm really sorry that I had to put you thru all of this. I promise next semester I'm going to work harder to get good grades.

I looked at the scedule you had me make last week, it is obvius my problem was, T.V. My schedule shows from Sunday to Thursday I spent watched T.V. 7 hours. I think if I cut down this waste, you will notice a change in my grades. The second item that ate up my time, visiting with friends. During this same time I spent 5 hours visiting with friends. That is over one hour a day. Another thing was basketball practice, this took up 4 hours but if possible I hope you'll let me stay on the team. A couple good things I did were I didn't spend much time on the phone, and also went to bed erly. Basketball is realy important to me, my friends are too. I like the idea of playing about the same amont of basketball and visiting my friends. I think I should be allowed to. So I think I should take a time each night and every night just for homework that way I could still be able to do basketball and watch some t.v. while getting good grades.

I think that if I do these things, my grades would go up and youd be proud of me.

Your son,
Andrew

Scoring Model for Exposition: Problem-Solution Essay

Score 1

This writer's attempt to produce an effective problem-solution essay is unsuccessful.

Problem Points:

1. Informal language unsuitable to audience
2. No stated solution
3. No elaboration of ideas
4. Unclear organization
5. Run-on sentences
6. Mechanical errors

Letter to the Mayor

Dear Mayor Adams,

  We have a problem for you to solve. I hope you will read this letter and pay attention to what I am saying, maybe you can come to our high school and talk to us about the issue which is so important to many of us students. The school is on the busiest street in the city and the traffic police we have is abcent a lot. Others try to help with the street crossing situashon but can't so there is a lot of confushun, like everyday kids almost getting hit crossing the street. Its always the same kids running across the street and the cars screech to a stop while the nose is awful. When there is police there we hav to walk in a single line like kinergardeners. Nobody can stand this and many students choose to cross the street any where but where they are suposed to, don't you think this is a problem. The teachers say they can't solve it, we hope you will solve it.

Sincerly,

Charles Anderson

Scoring Model for Research: Documented Essay

Score 4

This writer presents an essay with well-organized, documented information and a strong conclusion.

Strong Points:

1. Clearly stated thesis statement
2. Documented sources
3. Consistent organizational strategy
4. Researched information well integrated into essay
5. Elaborates main points
6. Very few mechanical errors

Fate of the Biggest Cats

At the beginning of last century, experts estimate that 100,000 tigers lived in the wild. Today, that number has shrunk to less than 6,000. This disastrous decrease in tiger population is the fault of human hands. (Tilson). Other than humans, the tiger has no natural predators, which gives the true source of the tigers' endangerment (Tilson).

To understand why tigers are becoming extinct, one must first understand the tiger's living habits and environment. First of all, the tiger lives in a variety of habitats, which range from the tropical forests of southern Asia to the woodlands of Siberia ("Tigers in the Wild"). Tigers also thrive in the mangrove swamps of the Sunderbans and dry, thorn forests of northwestern India. They live on a strictly carnivorous diet, which includes nearly all herbivorous mammals in the area. Their primary prey, however, is elk and wild boar. In some areas of Russia, their prey is unevenly distributed and moves seasonally, providing another challenge to these amazing creatures. As a result, their territory can range anywhere from one hundred to four hundred kilometers (Tilson).

Poaching, habitat loss, and population fragmentation pose the three main threats to tigers (Tilson). Even though laws prohibit the killing of tigers, poachers ignore the laws and continue to hunt the tigers. The poaching of tigers for their skins is an ancient practice; the beautiful striped fur has long been in demand for rugs, decorative wall hangings, and priceless coats. Although they cost thousands of dollars, tiger skin coats remain extremely popular in many Asian countries. Many Asian countries provide a constant demand for tiger bones, tails, whiskers, eyeballs and other body parts for use in traditional medicines (Jackson). According to folklore, the eyeballs are used to treat epilepsy; the tail for various skin diseases; whiskers for toothaches; the brain for laziness and pimples (Mills). Of all the tiger parts, the bone itself is the most commonly used. Tiger bones contain calcium and protein, which clinical research indicates to have an anti-inflammatory effect in animals with arthritis (Mills).

Habitat loss also threatens the tiger. When people cut down forests in the wild, the animals lose their homes and have trouble finding their prey. As a result, they begin to eat the livestock of near-by villagers. Sometimes they even eat people. Villagers often kill the tigers to protect their own lives and their livestock (Tilson).

Population fragmentation interferes with normal tiger reproduction. As the human population grows, it expands farther into the tiger's natural environment; villages and farms separate groups of tigers from each other. This prevents tigers in one area from mating with tigers in another area; therefore, they mate in the same small groups. Over time, inbreeding weakens the gene pool, leaving many baby tigers with mutations (Tilson).

As with many of the world's problems, the extermination of tigers can stop if enough people become involved. Authorities say they have no way to enforce the illegal killing of tigers because too few people become involved in the effort. Concerned persons must volunteer to help understaffed police agencies in order to catch and apprehend those guilty of poaching. Until more people become involved, these beautiful creatures will continue to diminish in number, and future generations may never have the opportunity to see them anywhere except in pictures.

Works Cited

Jackson, Peter. "Species in Danger." March, 1998. http://www.Tigereyes.com/ (January 25, 2000).

Mills, Judy. "Killed for Medicine." August, 1994. http://members@aol.com (January 24, 2000).

Smith, Janet. "Tigers Running to Extinction."*National Geographic.* January, 1997: 61–68.

"Tigers in the Wild." January, 1998. www.panda.org/ (January 25, 2000).

Tilson, Ron. "Threats to Tigers." August, 1999. www.5tigers.org/ (January 25, 2000).

Scoring Model for Research: Documented Essay

Score 3

This documented essay has a clear thesis statement with well-documented supporting details and citations.

Strong Points:

1. Purpose identified in thesis statement
2. Statements supported with documentation
3. Researched content integrated into the writing
4. Details from documented sources

Problem Points:

1. Some questionable or unsupported content
2. Weak conclusion
3. Some mechanical errors; run-on sentences
4. No separate listing of "Works Cited"

The Crippler

The Polio virus is a disease that has existed for thousands of years. Since the Middle Ages, doctors have struggled to find a cure for this crippling virus, it has only recently been found.

Poliomyelitis has many names, including Polio and Infantile paralysis. Polio is an acute communicable disease caused by the polio virus. Cases can be as severe as fatal paralysis or as minor as an inapparent infection *(Professional Guide to Diseases Sixth Edition* 234).

Poliomyelitis once occurred in infants and children, but today is most common in people over the age of 15. Adults and girls are at more risk for infection, boys are more likely to be paralyzed. Pregnancy, old age, and localized trauma are factors that increase the risk of paralysis. About 85 percent of children who are infected with the virus have no symptoms at all *(The American Medical Association Encyclopedia of Medicine* 806).

The polio virus has three viruses found worldwide, they are transmitted from person to person by direct contact. The incubation period ranges from 5–35 days. The polio virus comes into the body through the alimentary tract, it then multiplies in the oropharynx and in the lower intestinal tract. After it multiplies, it spreads to the lymph nodes and to the blood *(Professional Guide to Diseases Sixth Edition).*

Inapparent poliomyelitis accounts for 95 percent of all infections. Minor illness is 4–8 percent of all cases, this polio causes a slight fever, malaise, headache, sore throat, inflamed pharynx, and throwing up. The infected person usually recovers in about 72 hours.

Major poliomyelitis involves the central nervous system. It has two forms, nonparalytic and paralytic. *(The American Medial Association Encyclopedia of Medicine.)*

Paralytic poliomyelitis has symptoms like a moderate fever, headache, vomiting, lethargy, irritability, and pains in the neck, back, arms, legs, and abdomen, constipation, weakness in different muscles, and hypersensitivity to touch. The extent of paralysis depends on the level of spinal cord lesions *(Professional Guide to Diseases Sixth Edition).*

Sometimes the poliomyelitis affects the brain, then it is called bulbar paralytic poliomyelitis the most crippling type. This form affects the respiratory nerves, which could lead to paralysis of the lungs *(Professional Guide to Diseases Sixth Edition* 235).

In 1840 poliomyelitis was an epidemic in Norway and then in Sweden in 1905. During the first half of this century, out breaks showed up in Europe, North America, Australia, and New Zealand. Today, minor polio outbreaks occur mostly in non-immunized groups like the Amish people in Pennsylvania. The disease usually strikes during the summer and fall *(Professional Guide to Diseases Sixth Edition* 235).

Poliomyelitis control was made possible when in 1949, the American bacteriologist John Franklin Endears and his coworkers discovered a method of growing the viruses in the laboratory. Using this technique, the American physician and epidemiologist Jonas Salk made a vaccine prepared from viruses of the three known types. After field trials in 1954, the vaccine was pronounced safe and effective, "mass inoculation" began. It has now been rightly called a miracle drug of modern medicine. The vaccine contains dead polio viruses that force the body to make antibodies to polio. "The vaccine so effectively eliminated poliomyelitis that today it's hard to appreciate how feared the disease once was" *(Professional Guide to Diseases Sixth Edition* 235). Today the Sabin vaccine can be taken orally, it is more than 90 percent effective. There is no effective drug treatment for polio.

Scoring Model for Research: Documented Essay

Score 2

This writer presents a documented essay whose problems outnumber its strong points.

Strong Points:

1. Some documentation
2. Elaboration

Problem Points:

1. No clear thesis statement
2. Inconsistent organizational strategy
3. Too many details; repetitious ideas
4. Loosely integrated research; only one documented source
5. Numerous mechanical errors
6. No conclusion

Portrait of Author

Frances Hodgson Burnetts book *The Secret Garden* was very intresting to me. The plot was nothing like I had read before. I thought it would be interesting to find out about her life and other books she had written, she didn't seemed like no ordinary author.

The first experience that had a major affect on Frances Hodgsons life was coming to America from England. She was 15 and her uncle wrote to her mother to bring the children to Knoxville, Tennessee, and hed find jobs for the boys. Frances mother knowed this would be better for there family so she agreed. It seemed like she'd never see England again but she went 32 more times in her life.

Frances Eliza Hodgson was born fifteen years before, on November 24, 1849 the middle of five children. Frances lived in England in her early years. Her family moved to America at 15 just after Abraham Lincoln's assassination. Frances Eliza Hodgson moved around a lot in her lifetime but her home was in Boston. She often went to England.

The entire trip to America took 5 weeks. 3 weeks by ship to Quebec, Canada and 2 weeks by train to Tennessee. Times in Tennessee were bad because of the war. Her mother and Frances and her two younger sisters moved to a log cabin in New Market. Frances spent many hours with her next door neighbor Swan Burnett the son of the local doctor. Frances started writing and often shared her stories with her younger sisters.

Frances married Swan Burnett on September 19, 1873 in New Market at the Burnett family home and was blessed with two boys named Lionel and Vivian. Vivien was a girl's name but a popular novel had a male character named Vivian, and Frances changed the spelling, and she used it for her son. In the spring of 1889, Frances sailed for Europe with her son Vivian and Lionel stayed in Washington with his father. Lionel fell ill. The whole family had caught the flu that winter. Vivian recovered quickly but Lionel had relapses and Frances received many letters with bad news because Lionel did not have the flu, but tuberculosis.

Frances sailed home refusing to believe that her son was dying. When she saw him she made a special effort to be cheerful as if he would soon be well. Lionel died quietly on December 7, 1890. Frances wrote to her cousin "Early in the morning he coughed a little, when the nurse bent over him she knew the end had come." (*Beyond The Secret Garden*, Page 77).

Some of Frances's feelings toward her son were put into her book *In the Closed Room*. After ward, Frances writes many more books. Frances rents a country house in England and makes it her new home and the garden becomes her outdoor study and later she used her garden to write her second best seller, *The Secret Garden*. Her first best selling book being *Little Lord Fauntleroy*. Frances had a hobby of dressing herself up even if she were to stay indoors. I never pictured her as a fluffy, frilly person. However, she must have been since her nicknames included Fluffy, Fannie and Flufina.

Works Cited

Carpenter, Angelica Shirley and Jean Shirley. *Frances Hodgson Burnett—Beyond the Secret Garden*. Minneapolis: Lerner Publications Company, 1990.

Scoring Model for Research: Documented Essay

Score 1

This is an unsuccessful attempt at writing a documented essay.

Problem Points:

1. No thesis statement
2. No citation of reference works
3. No documentation incorporated into essay
4. Lack of fluency
5. Awkward sentence construction
6. Many errors in spelling, usage, and mechanics
7. No conclusion

A Bleeding Disese

Hemophelia is a blood cloting problem you get in your genes. Mostly men get it. 400 babies a year are born with the disease with the male children being the mostly likely to get it. There are 20,000 of them in the US. Its called different names because its the oldest bleeding disease you can inherit, some other names are Christmas disease and factor 1X. Hemophelia can be very painful. Hemophelacs blood don't clot right. And hemophelia has less causes and a lot of symptoms, there is also some treatments, for the patent.

There is a couple of causes of hemophelia, many symptoms, and a blood test to tell you got it. You can get hemophelia in an inheritence and also by low blood proteen. You cant catch hemophelia but a person can get it from blood contact and also intestin tract bleeding. Other symptoms are also headakes, sleeping, throwing up, and confusion. Hemopheliacs bleed internally and in many areas of the body and they even bleed in thier musles. Musles swell from bleeding and makes the nerves num. The worst pain comes when the joints bleed and swell. When Hemopheliacs grow up there joints bleed more. Hemopheliacs can die from cuts and surgury. There is treatments for Hemophelia and good outcomes, there is also perventions.

Hemophelia hasn't no cure but you can treat it. Its treated by infutions. Novoseven is a pill for Hemopheliacs but just Hemophelia A. But medicines are being made for infution and people can take them at home but they are very expensive and sometimes is not enough. Hemopheliacs can stop the bleeding by taking an injecsion. There is also perventions like genetic treatments. Other facts are that Hemopheliacs have to be careful but they can be normal but should not play contact sports. Hemophelia can cause bad arthritis and baby hemopheliacs are safe until they start walking.

Scoring Model for Research: Research Paper

Score 4

This writer successfully creates a research paper with a clear thesis statement, strong supporting details, and clear organization.

Strong Points:

1. Clearly stated thesis
2. Complete citations
3. Logical oganization
4. Conclusions drawn from research
5. Overall clarity and fluency in writing
6. No mechanical errors

Down Syndrome

Despite all the myths and superstitions, Down syndrome does not discriminate among its victims. It affects men and women equally (Down[1] 987), in all races, social, and economic classes, and all countries (Cunningham 84). Down syndrome, the most common type of mental handicap (Down's[3] 436), affects one in a thousand people. There are 250,000 people in the United States suffering from Down syndrome (March 1). The average intelligence (IQ) of a Down syndrome person is 60 to 70 (Down's[2] 435). The average life span of a person with Down syndrome is 55 years (March 1). Sadly enough, Down syndrome lasts for a person's whole life (Down's[3] 1).

In 1886, Langdon Down, a British physician and early champion for the mentally handicapped, discovered Down syndrome, at that time called mongolism. Later the disease would be named after him (Wynbrant 90 102).

Down syndrome, scientifically called trisomy 21 (Down's[3] 1), is a chromosomal abnormality causing mental retardation and other physical abnormalities (March 1). This disease has numerous causes and a variety of symptoms.

In normal humans, when a sperm and egg cell unite, 23 pairs of chromosomes are created, 46 chromosomes in all (Pueschel 43–45). In people with Down syndrome, something abnormal occurs in the creation of certain pairs of chromosomes, and it is usually a third copy of chromosome 21. This condition is called trisomy 21.

Down syndrome symptoms include such physical abnormalities as an asymmetrical skull (Down[2] 1), speckling in the iris (Wynbrant 103), a fold of skin on the inner corner of the eye called the epicanthal fold (Cunningham 89), crossed eyes, near or far sightedness, cataracts (March 1), Mongolian slanted eyes, short hands with short broad fingers (Down's[3] 1), small ears, flat nasal bridge, a large tongue with a small mouth, distinctive creases on the hands and feet, a malformed fifth finger (Down[1] 987) being double-jointed (March 1), a wide space between the first and second toes (Down[1] 987), and round cheeks.

Although there is no cure for Down syndrome, there are different treatments. For example, there are antibiotics for certain infections, glasses for vision correction, surgery for heart defects, hearing aids for poor hearing (Down[1] 988), and plastic surgery to correct the eyes and cheekbones (Cunningham 105).

In addition, there are treatments to help the emotions of people with Down syndrome. Down syndrome children need extra care and attention. People must be sure not to criticize them (Down's[3] 436). There are groups in communities that help family and friends of a Down syndrome child deal with emotions.

In addition, the Down syndrome child should mix with normal children as well as with children having the same handicap, and adults should stimulate the child's senses and allow the child to develop at his or her own pace

(Down's[2] 436–437). Many people with Down syndrome can attain a high level of achievement, and whenever possible, they should be allowed and encouraged to do so. The television actor Chris Burke is one outstanding example. Growing up, he had great encouragement from his family, and he often referred to his condition as "Up Syndrome" rather than Down (Arc). Special Olympics contestants are other excellent examples of the levels Down syndrome people can reach.

Fortunately, with the recent isolation of the genes encoded in chromosome 21, researchers are able to identify the genetic sequencing and organization of this chromosome and hope for a genetic breakthrough to prevent Down syndrome. On the medical front, advances in health care are enabling individuals with the condition to live longer and to function more independently than ever before. In conclusion, Down syndrome is a complex disease, but medical interventions and genetic research may lead to a cure.

Works Cited

The Arc of Arkansas. "Biography of Chris Burke." http://www.arcark.org/burke.html.

Cunningham, Cliff. *Understanding Down's Syndrome.* Cambridge: Brookline Books, 1996.

"Down's Syndrome." http://www.Adam.com.ency/article100997.htm 7 Jan 2000

"Down's Syndrome." *Encyclopedia of Family Health.* 1998 ed.

"Down syndrome." *The Gale Encyclopedia of Medicine.* 1999 ed.

"Down syndrome."http://www.healthanswers.com/centers/topic/overview.Asp?id=children's+health&filename=000997.htm 7 Jan 2000

"Down's Syndrome." http://health.excite.com/content/dmk/dmk_article_1457373 6 Jan 2000.

"March of Dimes Down syndrome." http://www.noah.cuny.edu/pregnancy/march_of_dimes/birth_defects/downsynd.html#What%20is%20Down%Syndrome 7 Jan 2000.

Pueshel, Siegfried M. *A Parent's Guide to Down Syndrome.* Baltimore: Paul H. Brooks Publishing Company, 1990.

Schiender, Dan. "The Heart and children with Down Syndrome." *The Tidewater Down Syndrome Association Newsletter.* 12 Jan 2000.

Wynbrant, James and Mark D. Ludman. "Down's Syndrome." *The Encyclopedia of Genetic Disorders and Birth Defects.* 1991 ed.

Scoring Model for Research: Research Paper

Score 3

This research paper has logical organization and appropriate support data.

Strong Points:

1. Clearly stated conclusion
2. Logical, organized paragraphs
3. Good factual details

Problem Points:

1. More sources should be cited in last half of paper
2. Some mechanical and grammatical errors

Influenza

Each year, millions of people come down with the symptoms of the flu, fever, runny nose, joint aches, and vomiting. Pharmaceutical companies make billions of dollars marketing drugs to relieve the symptoms. A modern day inconvenience, the influenza virus has been around for thousands of years when it was so powerful, it brought down an entire civilization.

The sickness came to Athens in the year 431 B.C. For more than a year, the epidemic raged. Thucydides, a scholar in Athens, was its chronicler (Kolata 35). The symptoms of this epidemic, later called influenza, were frightening, strong and healthy people would suddenly get "violent heats in the head, redness and inflammation in the eyes, sneezing, and hoarse voices," Thucydides wrote in his historic account of the city.

One of the earliest descriptions of the flu written 2500 years ago, by the Greek physician Hippocrates, outlined the popular theories of the time. The flu was described as having a number of different causes including "bad air" and several kinds of bacteria. It wasn't until 1933 that the cause was correctly identified as a virus (Barrett 12).

There have been several other major influenza epidemics in the history of the world. An outbreak in Europe in 1556 lasted four years, and had serious consequences, in some cities in Europe. As much as 20 percent of the population was wiped out (McNeill 16).

A more recent outbreak occurred in 1918. Lasting only a year. No one knows for sure where it came from or how it turned into such a killer. All that is known is that the virus that infected people in the spring of 1918 started out as a mild strain with very few serious cases. The strain vanished only to reappear in the fall, killing an estimated 20–100 million people.

Even today, with the advances in molecular biology and in the pharmaceutical industry, viral infections—influenza in particular—are largely untreatable. Medical researchers have known for decades that the simple influenza virus has only eight genes, and that the virus dies within hours if left alone with no new cells to infect. Researchers know that the influenza virus infects only the cells of the lungs. But the critical information that researchers have been unable to figure out is how to make a medicine that is the equivalent of penicillin for the flu (Kolata 27).

The treatment for flu symptoms hasn't changed much since Thucydides first recorded his observations. Doctors still recommend drinking plenty of fluid and getting lots of rest. For a more severe case of the flu drugs can be prescribed, but won't destroy the virus itself, vaccinations are recommended each season. Especially for older people. However this is not a perfect solution as there are many strains of the flu, each vaccine can only combat one strain.

Medical advances have redirected the influenza virus from a widespread scourge to a mere inconvenience. But until a drug can be developed that will effectively kill the virus, the flu will continue to be a part of society worldwide.

WORKS CITED

Barrett, Julia. "Influenza." *Gale Encyclopedia of Medicine.* 1999 ed.

Kolata, Gina. *Flu.* New York: Farrar, Straus and Giroux, 1999

Unknown. Relief from Flue Symptoms [Online] Available http://www.lahealthcare.com/cond/flu/relief.html. 1997–2000

Unknown. Treatment [online] Available http://lahealthcare.com/cond/flu/treat.html. 1997–1998.

Scoring Model for Research: Research Paper

Score 2

This writer presents an organized research paper, but the paper's weaknesses outnumber its strengths.

Strong Points:

1. Appropriate facts, examples, and details to support main points
2. Logical organization

Problem Points:

1. Unclear thesis statement
2. Incomplete and insufficient citations
3. Little variety in sentence structure
4. Usage and mechanical errors
5. Abrupt ending; lacks conclusion
6. Works Cited out of alphabetical order

Warm Up

One of the most dangrous threats to our Earth is strengthening every second. Slowly, molecules that exist in the air are smothering the atmusfear. This phenomenon is affecting the Earth's natural heating and cooling system. This ocurence has left scientists worried for years, they can't predict what will happen next or how to fix the problem. Different theories have been presented, only time will tell if any of them will help.

The "Green house Affect" is the name of the Earth's temperture control sistem, it keeps the Earth just warm and cool enogh to suport life. Without it life would not exist here. This sistem is made up of the ozone layer that acts as a sheild against harmful rays trying to enter Earth's atmusfear, this barrier allows heat from the sun to enter. And some infrared partikles escape. The remaning heat returns to the Earth and bonces around in the atmusfear as in a greenhouse the Earth is heated in this manner. That is "Greenhouse Affect" came about *("What is the Greenhouse Affect?")*.

The problem is that certain molecules in "greenhouse gases" destroy the ozone and harmful stuff enters the atmusfear and the Earth keeps getting warmer. This is "Global Warming." It could be a serious in the future *("Page 1")*.

"Greenhouse gases" are made up of many diffrent gases, such as methane. This leds us to beleive that humans are to blame for the harming of the ozone. Methane is in diffrent things such as car exhaust *("New Scientist Global Warning Report")*. So there are many ways that these harmful gases can get into the air.

The temperture of the Earth is rising little by little and. flooding could leave millions homeless and farmland underwater. A shortage of food or even famin would sweep across some low lying countries *("EPA Global Warming Site")*. If no percautions are taken, the problem could *worsen* *("What is the Greenhouse Affect?")*.

Although an aparent problem exists, some say global warming could achually have a posative affect on the Earth. These rising tempertures could cause more carbo dioxite which helps trees grow and benifits people. *("New Scientist Global Warming Site")*.

Works Cited

"New Scientist Global Warming Report: All You Ever Wanted to Know. www.Newscientist.com/ nsplus/insight/global/faq.html (18 January 2000)

"EPA Global Warming Site." 12 January 2000. epa.gov/globalwarming/ (18 January 2000).

"Ozone Reality Check." 30 December 1999. www.foe.org.ozone/intro.html (18 January 2000).

"What is the Greenhouse Effect? 30 December 1999. www.tip.net.au/ ~edmondsgreenhouse/whatis.html (18 January 2000).

"What They Are." 30 December 1999 www.hab.com/hsbcfc2.htm (18 January 2000).

"Page 1." 7 October 1998. www.sacred.sf.ca.us/ces/a999/7grade/hamilton/ pag1.htm (18 January 2000).

Scoring Model for Research: Research Paper

Score 1

This writer's attempt to write a research paper is unsuccessful.

Problem Points:

1. No thesis statement
2. No list of reference works
3. Disorganized presentation of information
4. Irrelevant and repetitious information
5. Unsupported opinions
6. No conclusion
7. Numerous usage and mechanical errors

Green, Green, Green

Everybody has a favorite coler. It is your own decision. Colers are used in everyday life. Starting at clothes and working itself all the way to U.S. dollar bills. Green, why was green chosen to be the coler that every U.S. citizen touches and sees everyday. Is the coler green some how special or is it some famus person's faverite coler or is it just a cheap coler.

Green is a dull coler which doesn't really catch your eye. Unless you see the coler green on a doller bill. Was green chosen because the president or someone famous at the time like the coler. There have been many Presidents who like the coler green. But it's not chosen because it was some Presidents faverite coler. Even though green was the faverite coler of John Quincy Adams, Ronald Ragan, and George Bush. Will Smith, Katie Homes, Meg Ryan, John Wayne, Sean Connery, and Nicholas Cage all picked green as there faverite coler too. They are all famous people that everyone knows so maybe they picked the coler. Or maybe it was a star athlete like Barry Sanders or Joe Montana who like the dullness of green. Once again they are famus people, but they did not have a say on the coler pick neither. If the coler wasn't picked by a president or movie star or athlete, then there must be something special about the coler green.

There isn't really anything that is really special about the coler of green. The printing of money started at the Treasury Department's Bureau of Engraving and Printing. Here is where the pigments and colers are kept to make money. The coler was chosen because of the large amounts of the pigments at the time. If it was a decade or even a couple of years later would the coler be different. You could say that it was the timing that the coler was picked. When the pigment green was chosen to be the coler of our U.S. dollar bills it was a time where all kinds of pigments and colers were being used to make clothes, and tons of other things. Was it good or bad timing that left us with a life long coler to remember? The reason the dollar bill had to have coler was because of the high rate of counterfit money. Something needed to be done, and done quick. And so at that time is when green became the coler. So I guess if you like green it was good timing, but if you don't like it was bad timeing (Fitzel 62). The money could have been any coler, and if there was a higher quanity of another coler at the time it would of probably been a different coler. If the coler was different, what coler would look good?

Green has never been populer. It just isn't bright or bold. It is kind of dull, so people just don't like it. But greens popularity changed in 1929 when it was chosen for the coler of our money. You still may not like the coler, but you still have to see it everyday.

Scoring Model for Response to Literature

Score 4

This writer presents an articulate and well-supported response to literature.

Strong Points:

1. Effective use of background
2. Forceful presentation of ideas
3. Logical organization
4. Elaborated reasons and supporting examples
5. Overall fluency and clarity
6. Vocabulary
7. No mechanical errors

The Downfall of Macbeth

Shakespeare's play *Macbeth* is considered a great and important play. One reason for its popularity is its timeless theme—the downfall of a noble man, the highly respected Macbeth, due to his ambition and greed. This is still a common problem in our society. Every day there are new stories about politicians, actors, and athletes who lose everything through overwhelming ambition. In this essay I will discuss the downfall of Macbeth by comparing his character in the beginning of the play with his character toward the end of the play. I will also discuss who and what caused the downfall of this ill-fated leader.

Early in the play, Shakespeare alerts the reader to Macbeth's bravery. By letting a soldier tell about Macbeth's bravery and loyalty to King Duncan of Scotland, Shakespere makes Macbeth's reputation seem more reliable and impressive than if Macbeth himself spoke of the matter. The soldier tells how well Macbeth dealt bravely with a traitor. The soldier's statement is supported by a messenger's story. He tells the King that Macbeth and his best friend, Banquo, led the Scottish forces in the war against Norway. This helps establish Macbeth's greatness early in the play.

Yet Macbeth's character begins to change quickly. The process begins when three witches tell him that he will become King of Scotland. Before this, Macbeth would probably never have thought of being disloyal to his king, but something inside him "wakes up." The first serious sign of his character flaw is when he first contemplates the murder of King Duncan. He is very nervous about it and his conscience seems to bother him. But he steels himself for the act and soon has committed the deed. Unable to stop, he soon commits his second and third murders. He hires two murderers to kill his friend Banquo, as well as an innocent woman and her child. This is the climax of his character-change. After this he becomes "cold" and emotionless: "I have almost forgot the taste of tears . . . Direness, familiar to my slaughterous thoughts, cannot once start me" (Act 5, Scene 5, lines 10–14). He is now so cold that he is not even disturbed by the cry of women. Macbeth has changed from a brave, loyal and caring noble man into a disloyal and cold murderer.

It is hard to say who or what causes the drastic change in Macbeth's character. In my opinion there are several "forces" that motivate him. It is not until the witches make their prophecies that murdering the king even enters Macbeth's mind. But he starts thinking about this awful crime before his wife, Lady Macbeth, brings it up. That must suggest that he is not good all the way through, and that he is capable of thinking "bad thoughts." Even though the witches gave him a push in the wrong direction, and Lady Macbeth encourages him to commit the first murder, I think his own dark, power-hungry nature is the main "force" behind his change. He should not be influenced by others in such a way. Somewhere in him there must have been the ambition that would overrule his conscience and allow him to commit these terrible crimes.

The downfall of Macbeth is the main theme in Shakespeare's play. This character change is what makes the play a tragedy, which is defined as the downfall of a person of noble stature. These kinds of tragedies happen in our time, as well. Perhaps one could hope that we would have learned from the mistakes and tragedies of the past. But unfortunately, tragedies like Macbeth's still happen today.

Scoring Model for Response to Literature

Score 3

This writer presents a generally effective response to literature in an essay with some mechanical errors.

Strong Points:

1. Presents background information
2. Presents points in logical order
3. Reasoning supported with specific examples

Problem Points:

1. Several instances of faulty usage
2. Some unclear reasoning
3. Some mechanical errors

Fair Is Foul and Foul Is Fair

Sometimes life throws up obstacles that seem to make success impossible. These obstacles are often so deceptive in their appearance that we don't recognize them until they cause our demise. Shakespeare understood deception in life and touches on this timeless concern in his plays. This motif in *Macbeth* is summed up in an interesting paradox that also captures the confusion and despair felt by people today, "Fair is foul, and foul is fair." I will discuss how this paradox was the case in *Macbeth*.

The motif is first introduced with the appearance of the three witches in Act I, Scene 1, line 10. The witches declare their prophecies and convince Macbeth of their abilities. He is astounded when they know his name and accurately foretell that he will become Thane of Cawdor. These witches, however ugly and sinister they may be must appear fair to Macbeth in some respects. They clearly have great powers and, the notions they put in his head are seductive ones. Macbeth clearly embraces their predictions. What they say appears to bode well for Macbeth but, in truth their prophecies will spell doom for the man. The witches exemplify foul being fair.

Another excellent example of foul appearing fair is seen in King Duncan's reign, beginning with the treachery of the first Thane of Cawdor. This thane appeared to be a loyal subject to the king but, is discovered to be a traitor. Later, King Duncan rewards Macbeth with a high honor by naming him Thane of Cawdor and, further honors him by staying at Macbeth's home. Having served as a just king and having treated these men honorably, Duncan deserves to be treated honorably in return. For all appearances, Macbeth will serve Duncan well. Yet Duncan's fair deeds are foully repaid. Macbeth kills Duncan while he is sleeping as a guest in his home. This is an atrocious act, as Macbeth himself acknowledges near the end of Act I: "He's here in double trust: / First, as I am his kinsman and his subject . . . / Then as his host / Who should against his murderer shut the door, / Not bear the knife myself." By presenting the reader with these betrayals, Shakespeare is driving home his point that, all too often, "fair is foul and foul is fair."

A final example of fair being foul is what happens to Banquo. He was very loyal to the king, even to the point of serving as a character foil for Macbeth. loyal to the king, even to the point of serving as a character foil for Macbeth. In lines 25–30 of Act II, Scene I, he says that he would gladly help Macbeth but not if he had to betray his conscience or his loyalty to his country. Macbeth also kindly asks Banquo to attend his feast when he is actually preparing to kill him. This good friend is rewarded with foul murder and a threat to his son's life. Fair is foul once again in Macbeth's kingdom.

The world often seems to have the theme of "Fair is foul, and foul is fair." How many of us, now and through the ages, have had to face this treacherous fact of life? Too often people are betrayed by friends, undone by ambition or, led astray by those we love, just as the characters in *Macbeth* are. The realism of this vision makes *Macbeth* piercing and timeless. Yet Shakespeare carries readers beyond this tragic realization. In the tragedy of *Macbeth* the ending suggests that foulness is indeed foul and, Macbeth receives his just rewards.

Scoring Model for Response to Literature

Score 2

Although this writer provides a response to literature in an organized format, its weaknesses in content and style outweigh its strengths.

Strong Points:

1. Some organizational structure
2. Some reactions supported with reasons and examples

Problem Points:

1. Lacks thesis statement and conclusion
2. Awkward and misleading terms
3. Lack of clarity
4. Poor organization at key points
5. Awkward sentence structure and style
6. Numerous mechanical errors

Themes in *Macbeth*

Upon reading Shakespeare's *Macbeth*, you can notice the repetition of several themes and symbols. The use of these greatly increases the overall affectiveness of the play. They include deceptive appearances, supernatural events, and the symbolic references to blood.

One important theme in *Macbeth* is when Shakespeare shows the deceptive nature of people and situations. Like where the witches claim that "Fair is foul, and foul is fair". In this way, the audience is warned from the beginning not to be mislead by pretences. Another time appearances are used to decieve is where Lady Macbeth is instructing her husband how to act when recieving Duncan. She tells him to "Look like the innocent flower / But be the serpent under 't" in Act I. A final example of this irony can be found the second time Macbeth visits the witches. All the things they tell him are seemingly unfeasable, yet throu the use of double meanings and carefully chosen words, these apparent impossibilities come quite true. These are just three instances where things are not as they seem.

A second repetition is the appearance of aparitions. There are three different supernatural events. First, just before Macbeth goes to murder the king. He sees a bloody dagger that leads him towards Duncan's room. The second example is the ghost of Banquo. This specter attends Macbeth's feast and reveals itself only to the host, much to Macbeth's horror and the guests' confusion. Another wierd encounter ocurs at Macbeth's second meeting with the witches. They conjur up aparitions that tell Macbeth of his future. All of these fantastic sights have a affect on the tragic hero.

Blood is refered to as a symbol of guilt from the beginning of the play to the end. For instance, Lady Macbeth convinces her husband that "A little water clears [them] of this deed." This means that once the blood is washed from their hands, the couple cannot be found guilty of wrongdoing. Little did she know that riding theirselves of this iniquity would not be so easy. Later, Macduff refers to Macbeth as a "bloody-sceptered" king. In the end, Lady Macbeth admits in her unconcious ramblings that she can never escape from her crimes. While she is sleep walking she dreams that she cannot cleanse her bloodstained hands.

Scoring Model for Response to Literature

Score 1

This writer's attempts to write a response to literature are unsuccessful.

Problem Points:

1. Scattered, disorganized structure
2. Little or no background information
3. Little forcefulness or clarity
4. Missing evaluative terms and expressions
5. Weak, confusing sentences reflecting incomplete thoughts
6. Mechanical errors

Macbeths Downfall

Shakespear's *Macbeth* contans a masterful plot that thickens with each scene. Serving as the perfect classic tragedy. The play leads its main character Macbeth down a dwindling road of personal flaws that dead ends with his death. Things that contribute to Macbeth's someone piteus downfall.

Macbeth begins his downward spiral because he cannot stand up to his wife's peer pressure. When faced with the decision of whether or not to assasinate King Duncan Macbeth came to the civilized decision to not get involved in no atrocity. But after a quick disgracing speech from Lady Macbeth he imediately caved under the pressure, this was the little push that sent Macbeth sliding down a downhill slope. He quickly metamorphosed into a different kind of person.

Macbeth's want to be king and his lust for power leads him to commit acts that he normally would be unreasonable to do. It was this ambition that merged with Lady Macbeth's peer pressure to result in the sleying of Duncan, time after time, Macbeth continually killed people he thought endangered his throne.

Believing and trusting in the witches' profecies was Macbeth's most fatel mistake. Their prediction that he would be king was the insiting force in the play. And led to the killing of Duncan. The profesies that Macbeth's reign would not until Birnam Wood moved to Dunsinane. No man of woman borne proved true and led to tragedy. The whitches predictions were both true and false, since they all had a loophole built in. Macbeth's confidence let him into a badly prepared for battle and his death was a direct result of this false confidence.

Scoring Model for Writing for Assessment

Score 4

This writer presents a well-organized comparison-and-contrast essay for assessment, with solid supporting details and few mechanical errors.

Strong Points:

1. Good thesis statement
2. Clear reason for comparison-and-contrast analysis
3. Generally clear, consistent organization
4. Elaborates ideas with facts, details, and examples
5. Links support information to comparison and contrast
6. Good sentence variety and vocabulary
7. Few or no errors in grammar, spelling, mechanics and usage
8. Clear conclusion

Tale of Two Cities

Although the United States is a large country with many different people scattered across the land, you can easily divide the country into just two regions—East and West. Within these two regions you can readily view the country in terms of just two cities—New York and Los Angeles. These two metropolises dominate the coasts of this country. The two cities are alike in some ways and dissimilar in others.

The charm of New York stems from its tight streets and tall high-rises, which still allow a sense of openness and freedom, despite their close proximity to each other. In contrast, the charm of Los Angeles emanates from its vastness and its sprawling sectors. On the other hand, the Big Apple and the City of Angels resemble each other in many ways. Both are home to a myriad of ideas and diverse ethnic and religious groups, offering something for everyone. Each has an identity of its own, yet both carry many of the same philosophies.

New York City has long been a symbol of America, both past and present. Since its inception, the city has played an important role in our nation's history and has remained on the cutting edge of national issues and interests. An old city, it was incorporated as New Amsterdam in 1653. The home of dozens of national news-broadcast stations and many international diplomatic offices in the United States, including the United Nations headquarters, New York is perhaps the single most important city in the United States and in the world.

As for the city itself, New York is often called "cramped" and "busy," though it still retains some openness. Although thousands of people and cars crowd the city, massive Central Park and dozens of open spaces provide alternatives to feeling "cramped." New Yorkers can also rise above the city by climbing the hundreds of skyscrapers.

New York City is a world leader in culture, finance, and commerce. It has long been the trendsetter in the nation, whether in hosting a world's fair, bringing home sports championships, or debuting stunning fashion apparel. Among its famous tourist attractions are Broadway, Wall Street, Coney Island, the World Trade Center, Times Square, the Empire State Building, Central Park, Park Avenue, Harlem, and Yankee Stadium. Cultural sites include the Metropolitan Museum of Art and the Metropolitan Opera House. The fame of New York obviously spans well beyond its city limits.

The fame of Los Angeles, though, should not be minimized. The largest city besides New York in the United States, Los Angeles is the cultural and entertainment capital of the nation. Unlike New York, which was founded by the Dutch, Los Angeles was populated in the eighteenth century by Spaniards and Mexicans. Today, as in New York, hundreds of different ethnic groups influence the culture of Los Angeles. As for fame in entertainment, there is no doubt that Los Angeles is king. It's the home of Hollywood, prosperous recording industries, and thousands of motion picture, television, and radio celebrities.

Unlike New York, Los Angeles uses space by going horizontally across the land. Unlike New York, Los Angeles does not have a subway system so automobiles are essential. Los Angeles' freeway system is one of the most remarkable human achievements in the world. Like New York City, Los Angeles has many world-famous landmarks, such as sandy beaches and the shops of Rodeo Drive and Melrose. Entertainment hot spots include Disneyland, Dodgers Stadium, Griffith Park, and the Hollywood Walk of Stars.

In conclusion, despite the distinctly different personalities of Los Angeles and New York, the politics, culture, commerce, material wealth, and landmarks of the two cities are very similar. As leaders of the nation, the two cities must maintain their individuality but recognize their similarities.

Scoring Model for Writing for Assessment

Score 3

This presents an autobiographical narrative for assessment that makes clever use of analogy and is generally clear and well-organized.

Strong Points:

1. Purpose stated clearly in introduction
2. Adequate elaboration with examples and details
3. Carefully chosen vocabulary
4. Solid organization

Problem Points:

1. Unclear relevance of some statements
2. Weak transitions
3. Some mechanical errors

The Harvest of Time

The bamboo tree is a very unique plant. Farmers carefully water and cultivate the seed for five years with absolutely no visible result. In the fifth year, though, in just a matter of weeks, a stalk appears and shoots to as much as 120 feet. It is curius that the bamboo varies so greatly from the normal growing pattern of plants, but then the bamboo is not exactly your ordinary tree.

Like the bamboo tree, I required years (about eleven) of cultivation before the first shy but hopeful shoots of a personality appeared through the stiffling soil of independence in which I had planted myself. Until the seventh grade, I had limited myself to two close friends. I see now that I was intimidated and to some degree taken advantage of as the youngest in the group, but when people think they are happy with what they have, they do not bother to look for something better. In the seventh grade, however, this small nucleus moved away, and I found myself asociating with more of my peers, this time on a more equal standing. Still, it was a few years more before truly fenomenal growth occurred. I still was unaware of the larger world beyond my small plot, not yet a true member of the forest community. Two years later, when in the ninth grade, I began attending a public school for the first time. Needless to say, it was quite a change from the small private school I had attended prevously. In such a large setting, there were no people that I saw often enough in a day to automaticly develop a friendship, and for the first time I had to seek and make friends without the aid of a schedule. It was difficult for a while. Over the summer between my sophomore and junior years, I realized that if I was to meet people, I must take action, either seeking them out or drawing them to myself. So finally, after two years of high school, I threw myself into life with the intensity of one aware of how much time he has already wasted. Somehow I saw what I should do and later I would see why. What initiated the stuning growth of the bamboo? It had different causes, but primarily it took the realization and admission that I was lonely, that, truthfully, "No man is an island." It took a special effort to break through the packed soil of reclussiveness (the soil was losened somewhat by a theatre arts class; I was now being graded on my interaction) and a spiritual watering in baptizm to give up the security of the self-focused ground and seek the skies. The effort was demanding, but now growth can and has begun. I realize, of course, I'm nowhere near my full "height," but I'll reach it very quickly. After that, there is no telling what this tree may become: a touching artist, a practical designer, or maybe a leader and inspiration to others. I can hardly wait.

Looking back, I'm truly stuned by how far I've come in these last few years. My awareness of myself and of others has grown. My motivation is finally taped. Above all, I've broken through the soil of my own shyness. I can feel the warm sunlight of caring for and being cared for by those around me. The glory and friendships are there for earning, and I plan to continue to bask and grow in them.

Scoring Model for Writing for Assessment

Score 2

This writer's autobiographical narrative for assessment is confusing and fails to engage the reader's interest.

Strong Points:

1. Contains characters and some dialogue
2. Conclusion expresses some reflection and personal growth

Problem Points:

1. Insufficient detail and elaboration
2. Confusing sequence of events
3. Ineffective transitions
4. Abrupt conclusion
5. Errors in grammar, punctuation, and spelling

Joey Learns to Swim

Well, it all started one Saturday morning 2 weeks after school let out. It was around seven in the morning when I was getting redy to go swim in our nearby indoor, city pool, my friend and I had decided 2 days ago to go on to the city pool that Saturday. I grabbed my towel, extra clothes and left. Outside, Dave, my friend was waiting on his bicycle. He yelled "What took you so long?" with an embarased voice I replied "Forget it let's go." I grabbed my bicycle laying on the grass and left.

We were on our way. Blocks away from my house we saw Joey, a third grader who was Dave's little brother who sometimes bugged us but not all the time. Joey asked us "can I come with you guys?" We laughed and said "you were going to the pool. You know you can't swim." Joey at that time felt depressed because he knew it was true but I guess he only wanted to hang around with us so right there I told Dave we should take him along to show him how to swim.

So Jocy went with us to the pool, as we got to our destination Joey was the first one to get ready. As we got ourselves in our suits and in the pool Joey was a bit scared we might let him drown. Dave calmed him down and made him go in with us. We showed him the basics like how to keep his breath, how to kick, after a long time of battling Joey how to swim he got the idea he was practaclly on his own from there. Joey, me, and Dave had fun all that afternoon swiming, playing, laughing, all of that. It was almost the perfect day sunny, cool water and Joey now knew how to swim. That afternoon when we were comeing from the pool Joey seemed glad he knows now how to swim.

I guess that's what I learned that day from Joey, and scince then I feel good about myself. People should start helping others, it brings a good feeling.

Scoring Model for Writing for Assessment

Score 1

This writer's efforts to write a comparison-and-contrast essay for assessment are unsuccessful.

Problem Points:

1. No reason for comparison-and-contrast analysis
2. Lacks organizational strategy and consistent focus
3. Analysis does not provide facts or examples to support comparison or contrast
4. Demonstrates poor and confusing use of language
5. Generates confusion
6. Many mechanical, grammar, and spelling errors
7. Lacks conclusion

America Compared to England
in the Seventeenth Century

May 22, 1634

Dear Brother,

The differecance between your country and this one is astonishing. There is so many diffenerances including, a chance to start over, ample amout of space, but most important religus freedom. But there is a negetive side too living in America, Im afraid such as strange foods and people, and having to start from scrach.

First of all, since Im living in America, I have a chance to start over. All my problems that I had in England are now gone. I have no more dets or enemies. I levet all my problems in England.

Further-more, There is so much space in America. In England l barely had a roof over my head, but here I have acers of land to choose from. Its beautiful contry out here. My family and I could build a grand house.

finally and the most crusal point, religous freedom. Here in America not all of us have to be one religon. It will be so nice to watch my children grow up in peace with nothing but pure people around them. But most important, they will be able to choose how they wish to worship.

On the other hand, This land is strange to me. Some of the food here is unlike anything Ive ever seen.

Finially, Id say the worse thing about coming to America would have to be that I have to start from scrach. I only have what is in my few bags and the cloths on my back to start over. But I do however have good tools and my husband is strong. I feel like we will be all rite.

I fear I must come to a conclusion, time is getting short. Think not one more thought of me for I will be fine, I love the country here and I feel my family and I will be very pleased here.

Sincerly,

Patience

Table of Contents

To the Teacher

Successful secondary education relies on continued open interaction with students and their parents. While you are the primary instructor, encouraging parents or guardians to take an active interest in their child's education in the following ways can help to reinforce the work that you do in the classroom:

- *Showing interest in a student's work and progress:* The interested parent validates the importance of school instruction, activities, and tests. Parents who provide support for students may also reinforce good study habits and encourage students to organize their time and get assignments done. In contrast, students whose parents are disinterested in their school work may learn to be disinterested as well.

- *Monitoring homework:* Parents who monitor homework can help students stay on task and keep up with the learning that has been introduced in class. In addition, parents are the first line of help. Parents who work with their children can help identify problem areas and deficiencies and encourage the student to seek further help. If a lesson or concept seems problematic, a parent could contact you to make appropriate plans.

- *Extending and/or enriching instruction:* When parents are aware of the specific content and concepts a child is learning, they are more likely to help the student make community connections or real-world applications. For example, when a student is learning to analyze media, a parent might initiate discussions about the television the family watches at home. Alternatively, when a student is learning about the Vietnam War or subsequent historic events, the parent might encourage the child to talk with relatives about their personal experiences or thoughts about the event.

As a teacher, you should take steps to build a good relationship with the parents and guardians of your students, such as the following:

- Sharing your state standards.

- Explaining the district's curriculum and assessment program.

- Encouraging parents to review the textbook.

- Providing timely, informative feedback about each student's assignments and progress.

The pages that follow offer you specific forms to establish and support the home-school connection.

Parent Welcome

Date: _____

Dear Parent or Guardian:

Recent studies show how important parental involvement is in helping students to achieve success in school. Because I know that you want your child to have an excellent year in English, I'm pleased to tell you about our curriculum and suggest some ways you can participate in improving your child's performance.

Our English textbook this year will be *Prentice Hall Literature: Timeless Voices, Timeless Themes*. This program combines a wide variety of quality reading selections with literature analysis, critical thinking and reading skills, and composition. Importantly, it connects the literature to students' own experiences through the development of themes relevant to students' lives.

You can help your child get the most from this program and from all of his or her homework by following this expert-tested advice:

- **Find the best time for studying.** Work with your teenager to decide on the best time for studying. Then, set that time aside at least five days out of every week. If there is no home-work, your child can use the time to review or plan ahead.
- **Eliminate common distractions.** Set aside a study area that is free from noise and other distractions. Turn off the TV. Your teenager may say that watching television is helpful, but no research supports this. In fact, watching television allows students to "turn off their minds" because it requires no action or interaction.
- **Avoid common interruptions.** Take messages if the telephone rings, and have your teenager alert his or her friends not to drop by during the established study time.
- **Provide physical conditions that help concentration.** Ensure that the study area has adequate lighting and is kept at a comfortable temperature. Provide a table or desk that has enough space for writing.
- **Keep supplies handy.** Keeping study materials nearby saves time. Placing them in a small bucket or box makes it easy to move them to the study area.
- **Encourage computer literacy.** Help your teenager to see the value of using the computer to write compositions and other assignments. Encourage your child to use the computers at home, school, or the public library.
- **Ask to see your child's books.** Looking through the books gives you a better idea of what your teenager is learning and shows him or her that you think the material is important.
- **Ask to see your child's work on a regular basis.** You do not need to criticize or regrade the papers—that will only make your teenager less willing to show you his or her work. Just let your child know you are interested.
- **Read.** By watching you read, your teenager will see reading as a valuable activity. You can be especially effective if you occasionally read and discuss one of the selections your child is covering in class.

I look forward to working with your child and hope you will contact me if you have any questions during the school year.

Cordially,

_____
English Teacher

Parent Letter:
Review of State Standards

Date: _____

Dear Parent or Guardian:

The state of _____ has established a set of English/Language Arts standards to ensure that all students in the state develop grade-level appropriate proficiencies in the Language Arts each year. I have attached the state standards to this sheet for your review. Please read, sign, and return this form. Feel free to indicate any questions or concerns you have. I will work to address any concerns you have about the instructional goals for this academic year.

Cordially,

_____
English Teacher

_____

I, the parent or guardian of _____, have reviewed the state standards in English/Language Arts for this academic year. I understand that these standards form the foundation for the instruction and educational expectations in the classroom.

_____
Parent

Please use these lines to indicate any questions, concerns, or comments you would like the teacher to address:

_____

_____

_____

_____

_____

_____

Parent Letter:
Selection Objectives and Standards Correlation

Date: _____

Dear Parent or Guardian:

In class, we are about to begin reading the following selection:

_____

The chart below indicates the selection objectives students will address, as well as the state standards that each objective develops.

Domain	Skill or Strategy	Standards Correlation
Reading		
Writing		
Written and Oral English Language Conventions		
Listening and Speaking		

These skills and strategies are intended to ensure your child's development in Language Arts. Please feel free to contact me if you have any questions.

Cordially,

_____

English Teacher

Parent Letter: Writing Home Review

Name _____ Date _____

To the Student: Fill in the name of a family member or an adult friend, and attach this letter to the final version of your work to request comments on your work.

Date _____

Dear _____,

    I am attaching something that I wrote in school recently. I would appreciate it if you would read it and tell me what you think of it. I am particularly interested in getting your answers to the questions below. You can answer them on the lines under each question.

What do you think my purpose is for writing this?

_____

Were you able to follow my thoughts? If not, where did you get lost? What could I have done to make it easier to follow along?

_____

Is there any information that you wish I had included? If so, what?

_____

_____

Are there any parts that you think I could have left out? If so, which parts?

_____

_____

What do you like best about what I have written?

_____

_____

What else would you like to tell me about what I have written?

_____

_____

    Thank you for your help.

Sincerely yours,

_____
Writing Student

Parent Letter:
Portfolio Home Review

Date _____

Dear _____,

    I am attaching a portfolio of work that I completed in school recently. I would appreciate it if you would review the contents and tell me what you think of my work. You can do this by answering the questions below. To help you, I have filled in the first few lines so you will know the purpose of this portfolio.

    I value your opinion very much. By sharing your response to my work with me, you will help me to learn and to make improvements in my next portfolio.

The purpose of this portfolio is to show _____

_____ .

Which item or items in the portfolio best support my purpose? What is it about them that strongly supports my purpose? _____

_____

Do any items in the portfolio seem weak or irrelevant? If so, which ones? What might I have done to strengthen them? _____

_____

Are there other things I might have included in my portfolio? How would they have helped? _____

_____

What else can you tell me about my portfolio? What suggestions would you offer for my next portfolio? _____

_____

    Thank you for your help.

Sincerely yours,

_____

Writing Student

To the Teacher: Have students attach this letter to their completed portfolios and use it to request comments on their portfolio from someone in the home.

Homework Log

Directions to the Student: Use this form to record your homework assignments in Language Arts each day. When you have finished each assignment, place a check in the *Completed* column. Ask your parent or guardian to sign the form at the end of each week.

Date	Assignment	Completed

Signature of Parent or Guardian _____

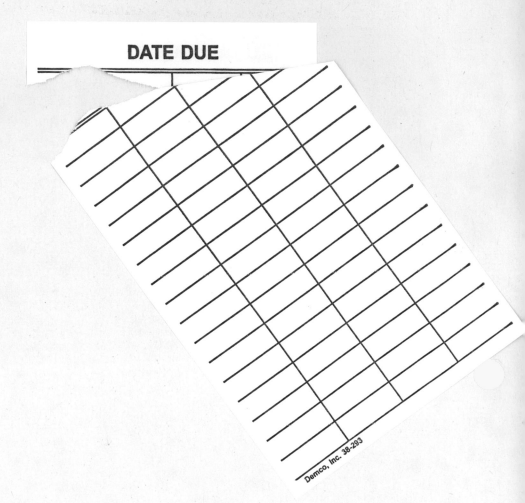

DATE DUE

Demco, Inc. 38-293